MAKIN(

Making Meetings Work is a short book which aims to help people chair
meetings better – meetings of all kinds from community playgroups
to conferences and dinners to large corporate Boards. The book is
based on the personal experience of a professional working chair
over many years. The book is aimed at younger men and women
who are beginning to chair their first meetings, and also at more
experienced chairs who want to develop their skills.

Richard Hooper has devoted his career to the technology, media
and telecommunications sector. He was a founder of the Open
University on the BBC side, developed with colleagues at British
Telecom the forerunner to the Internet – viewdata, and launched
one of the first satellite television channels – Superchannel. He was
founding deputy chair of the UK communications regulator Ofcom;
chair of Informa plc; and he chaired two reviews for Labour and
Conservative Governments on the Royal Mail and on copyright
licensing.

"Meetings are corporate ritual, a massive cost of time, talent and energy to any organisation. They are viral decay. This brilliant book explains how to stop viral decay, and stop it right now."

Simon Jenkins

"*Making Meetings Work: The Art of Chairing* is an essential guide for those who wish to chair meetings where no one feels left out or their opinions unheard. Richard chairs meetings like a great maestro conducting an orchestra. At the forefront of his mind are integrity, fairness as well as diversity. I am proud to have sat at the same table as him."

Baroness Floella Benjamin

"A decade ago Richard Hooper gave me a report on the future of the Royal Mail for the government. It was one of the best ever written. A decade later he has done it again, this time about how to make meetings shorter, more effective, more productive, and more enjoyable. What it lacks in jargon and business speak is made up for by his entertaining personal experiences and graveyard humour: the table used by the PM to chair Cabinet meetings in 10 Downing Street is, he is told by a civil servant, 'coffin-shaped. Everyone can see everyone.' There is even discussion of access to my 'ministerial biscuit tin'! The book is bang up to date with a final chapter on lessons from the pandemic – how to chair meetings in the modern digital era where even the biscuits are virtual."

Lord Peter Mandelson, *Co-Founder and Chairman, Global Counsel*

"[I]nspired guidance for successful meetings – essential reading for any Chair – new or experienced."

Stephanie Liston, *Chair Jersey Competition Regulatory Authority*

"Richard's book is simply excellent. It reflects the lifetime's work and learning of one of the most accomplished Chairs I have known. He shares many of the secrets that allow for the bringing together of differing views around a table and shows how to create full support for a strategy and its implementation. I will be recommending it to all my clients."

Stephen Bampfylde, *Founder and Partner, Saxton-Bampfylde*

"Hooper's mix of perceptive advice, practical tips and deep personal experience are a must read for anyone who wants to be In The Chair, rather than simply In The Room ... a well-written tome ... a well-written read."

Stephen Carter, *CEO Informa plc*

"One thing in life that we always have is our experiences. Sharing those experiences with others, and the insights and learnings you make, is a gift. This book is one such gift. It contains a lifetime of chairing experiences of all shapes and sizes in a succinct delightful and practical read. Whether you are chairing a small family or team meeting, or a public sector or large global company board, this handbook is gold for anyone who wants to make meetings purposeful, effective and fun."

Vanessa Oakley, *Executive General Manager Strategy & Business Operations, Chorus New Zealand Limited*

MAKING MEETINGS WORK

The Art of Chairing

Richard Hooper

LONDON AND NEW YORK

First published 2021
by Routledge
2 Park Square, Milton Park, Abingdon, Oxon OX14 4RN

and by Routledge
52 Vanderbilt Avenue, New York, NY 10017

Routledge is an imprint of the Taylor & Francis Group, an informa business

British Library Cataloguing-in-Publication Data
A catalogue record for this book is available from the British Library

Library of Congress Cataloging-in-Publication Data
Names: Hooper, Richard, 1939– author.
Title: Making meetings work : the art of chairing / Richard Hooper.
Description: Abingdon, Oxon ; New York, NY : Routledge, 2021. |
Includes bibliographical references. | Identifiers: LCCN 2020049587 (print) |
LCCN 2020049588 (ebook) | ISBN 9780367743024 (hardback) |
ISBN 9780367743031 (paperback) | ISBN 9781003157038 (ebook)
Subjects: LCSH: Business meetings. | Corporate meetings. | Meetings.
Classification: LCC HF5734.5 .H66 2021 (print) |
LCC HF5734.5 (ebook) | DDC 658.4/56–dc23
LC record available at https://lccn.loc.gov/2020049587
LC ebook record available at https://lccn.loc.gov/2020049588

ISBN: 978-0-367-74302-4 (hbk)
ISBN: 978-0-367-74303-1 (pbk)
ISBN: 978-1-003-15703-8 (ebk)

Typeset in Bembo
by Newgen Publishing UK

"All wise princes consider not only present but also future discords ... for being foreseen, they can be easily remedied. ... hectic fevers at their beginning are easy to cure but difficult to recognise, but in course of time when they have not at first been recognised and treated, become easy to recognise and difficult to cure."

(Niccolo Machiavelli, *The Prince*, 1532[1])

To Meredith my wife,

Who edits this my life.

To many friends and colleagues who have contributed

Thoughts, advice and quotes to this book.

To Rebecca Marsh and Sophie Peoples of Routledge/ Taylor & Francis

Who have produced this book.

And

To the people of Robe, South Australia

Who have looked after us during the plague year,

Allowing me to write this book.

"... it filled me with very serious thoughts of the misery that was coming upon the City, and the unhappy condition of those who would be left in it."
(Daniel Defoe, *A Journal of the Plague Year or Memorials of the Great Pestilence in London in 1665²*)

CONTENTS

CONTENTS

INTRODUCTION

The successful functioning of meetings depends upon thoughtful chairing.

Chairing meetings is seen as something that everyone can do. And everyone in *one* sense can chair a meeting – that is true. This book is about taking an everyday common-sense function like chairing a meeting and making it more "thought about", more practised and thus more effective.

I have been a working chair for many years, chairing many different types of meeting – Boards of large and small companies and of regulators; selection panels, conferences, dinners, Government reviews; family meetings, clubs and community organizations such as local playgroups and apartment block management companies. The suggestions here are based on personal experience of chairing and being chaired. In writing this book I have talked to Board directors, Board chairs and many friends and colleagues around the world who have contributed comments, thoughts and provided most helpful quotes. I have also been involved in mentoring aspiring and current Board directors, and in carrying out Board evaluations – both of which yield further insights into the process of chairing meetings.

This book thus brings together my experiences of chairing and being chaired and those of colleagues and contacts who have experience of chairing meetings across different sectors, both in the UK and beyond. It is deliberately short, the intention being to identify key lessons that can be applied within a short space of time to meetings you, the reader, are chairing or about to chair today or tomorrow. The book focuses on the practical points of chairing meetings and in this sense will, I hope, act as a useful guide and handbook. It does not, however, include tick-boxes and flowcharts, or Ten Commandments. Readers are encouraged to build their own conclusions and apply them to their own preferred ways of working. Different people will always chair in different ways, there is no one single "right" answer.

We can all be unhappy from time to time about the number and length of meetings we have to endure. Meetings are about opportunity cost. Time spent in meetings is time not spent elsewhere. The *New Oxford American Dictionary* describes opportunity cost as "the loss of potential gain from other alternatives when one alternative is chosen".[3]

Bartleby writing in *The Economist* said: "Most workers view the prospect of a two-hour meeting with the same enthusiasm as Prometheus awaited the daily arrival of the eagle, sent by the gods to pick at his liver".[4] Simon Jenkins in the *Guardian* savaged the notion of meetings with the heading:

The death of hope and productivity. We call it a meeting[5]

I first chaired meetings as a student at university – allocating finite theatre space to infinite demands from theatre people. My hope is that this short book might help to make chairing better, and thus improve the productivity of meetings. Perhaps even get some people to look forward to meetings as, I have to admit, I do. Most of the time.

Meetings are a fact of life in any organisation, public or private, large or small. This book seeks to be helpful to those who are chairing their first meetings, and to those who are already chairing and want to develop their skills. My aim is to help make meetings work better – both in business settings and in the wide range of settings other than business.

This book aims to offer practical tips based on my own and colleagues' practical experience. Hence the subtitle of the book – the art of chairing. A chair who studies the art of chairing will significantly increase the chances of having effective meetings. Practice is essential. Once a meeting is over, I think about where I could have improved, where I made avoidable mistakes. A very experienced and engaging CEO began a meeting he was chairing. He was presenting some key data on a television screen. The only trouble was that he stood slap in front of the television screen so we could not see the data. Blissfully unaware. No-one had the heart to tell him.

People should learn the skills of chairing as soon as they have the opportunity. Any chance to chair a meeting of any kind should be grasped as it is always an opportunity to learn more and get better. "The harder I practise, the luckier I get." Attributed to a number of professional golfers led by Gary Player.[6]

Conscious that anyone writing about management does so in fear of being critiqued as a jargon-dispensing bull-shitter, I have tried to make the advice about how to be a better chair as straightforward and as jargon-free as possible. Each chapter takes a particular type of gathering, starting with the ordinary everyday meeting in Chapter 1 and finishing in Chapter 9 with a PC (post-Covid) look at the future of chairing in an increasingly virtual, less physical world – which might or might not become "the new normal". Or, as one of my colleagues suggests, "the next normal".

VALUES

Values shape our approach to chairing. This book about chairing is founded on my personal belief that teamwork is a good thing and that consensus-driven (but not consensus-obsessed) decisions by a well-led, well-chaired group of people who trust each other are better than decisions taken unilaterally by one powerful person. And teams, meetings and Boards all work better if care and attention is paid to the diversity of people around the table, including the diversity of the chair her or himself (see Chapter 5).

Meetings should above all aim to make good decisions, based on good evidence and proper debate, in the interests of the organisations and all those who have a stake in the organisations, including of course the members of the meeting. That is what I mean by the title of this book "Making Meetings Work".

WORDS, WORDS, WORDS

The 13-volume 1933 *Oxford English Dictionary* (*OED*) usefully defines chairman as "the person who is chosen to preside over a meeting, to conduct its proceedings, and who occupies the chair or seat provided for this function". The word 'chairman' was first used in 1654. Under 'chairwoman', the 1933 *OED* notes haughtily that it is "hardly a recognized name" even though the first use of the word 'chairwomen' is surprisingly early – 1699. The *OED* also notes that the word 'chairwoman' is an obsolete form of 'charwoman' (that is to say cleaning lady).[7]

GOOD CHAIRS OF ALL GENDERS HAVE TO DO QUITE A LOT OF CLEANING UP – INSIDE AND OUTSIDE MEETINGS

For convenience, and to reinforce the emphasis on the need for diversity, in this book I have used the term 'chair', not 'chairman', 'chairwoman' or 'chairperson'.

I enjoy meetings. I enjoy chairing meetings and enjoy being chaired. I hope that the following pages will share that enjoyment.

REFERENCES

1. Macchiavelli, N. (2011), *The Prince*, London: Penguin Classics.
2. Defoe, D. (1959), *A Journal of the Plague Year*, London: Bestseller Library.
3. Flexner, S.B. (2001), *New Oxford American Dictionary*, Oxford: Oxford University Press.
4. Bartleby (30 June 2018), *The Economist*.
5. Jenkins, S. (14 September 2017), *Guardian*.
6. Player, G. (2002), *Golf Digest*, quoteinvestigator.com, accessed 14 July 2010.
7. *Oxford English Dictionary* (1933), Oxford: Oxford University Press.

1

CHAIRING A MEETING

The first thing that needs to be thought about is whether a meeting requires a chair. If the meeting is going to last more than a few minutes, handle issues of potential complexity and involve more than a few people, then it is worth having a chair.

There are three types of preparation that the chair needs to spend time on – the first is, for want of a better word, strategic; the second is technical; the third is being clear about meeting discipline.

PREPARING TO CHAIR – STRATEGIC ISSUES

The role of a chair in any meeting is, above all, to try and establish what needs to be discussed and what needs to be decided. Of course, there are meetings where the purpose appears to be, intentionally or unintentionally, to conceal or evade these two questions, leading to frustration, annoyance and railing against all meetings. The chair needs to develop in his or her mind an idea of what a successful meeting looks and feels like. So many meetings go on interminably because no-one is really sure what they are about. As a result, to mis-quote the first sentence of C. Northcote Parkinson's *Parkinson's Law,* meetings expand so as to fill the time available for their completion.[1]

The chair's tasks are the same generically for all types of meeting:

- to be clear what the meeting is about, what it is for and who it is for,
- to allow everyone attending (including the chair him or herself) a reasonable chance to give their views,
- to promote a sensible conversation or debate,

- to keep the meeting on track avoiding too many diversions,
- to keep track of time,
- to make, on behalf of the meeting, the necessary decisions without too much prevarication,
- to summarise what has been discussed and agreed,
- to emphasise the next steps,
- to finish the meeting as promptly and as early as possible,
- to ensure that, if appropriate, a record is kept of what was discussed and agreed; and who is responsible for the actions that have been agreed.

Above all else, the chair needs to be clear for whom and for what the meeting should work. The meeting should obviously work for those attending including the chair. But it also must work for the organisation, its goals and strategy and its responsibilities within the law towards a wide range of stakeholders – for example staff, shareholders, suppliers, customers, academics, local citizens, parents, club members, local communities. This is critical to the work of company Boards, as set out in Chapter 3.

The chair should also, where appropriate, try and ensure that the meeting has a warmth about it, and is enjoyable. Possibly even, for at least short periods, fun. One of the most successful Boards I served on was known for occasional howls of laughter emanating from the boardroom, to the quizzical amusement of staff sitting within earshot. As a result, staff invited to attend the Board for specific agenda items were less apprehensive and looked forward to coming.

People will come back willingly to subsequent meetings you chair if it has not just been a drudge. More importantly, people who are enjoying themselves, relax, and are more likely to trust each other and be honest with each other.

Who should come to the meeting? If we know what the meeting is for, it still can be spoilt by not having the right people in attendance. The chair must prepare by getting the right people to attend. If a key person is missing, either the meeting fails and/or you have to repeat it when that key person is available – not a very productive use of time.

Chapter 5 looks at the "right people" along the dimension of diversity – a major concern today for chairs in the make-up of teams, workforces and meetings. And a central concern for organisations is to ensure the diversity of chairs themselves. The word "diversity" in this book means a "good mix of genders, younger people, people from different ethnic and social class backgrounds, people with disabilities, people with different sexual preferences" (Chapter 5).

PREPARING TO CHAIR – TECHNICAL MATTERS

In preparation for a meeting, it is important to ensure that any technology required to enhance audibility and visibility is actually working. Too much time is still wasted in meetings when the PowerPoint presentation is not properly set up, for example, or the person presenting a topic is not sure which buttons to press. If there are going to be slides at the meeting, check, or get your team to check, that they are charged up and ready to go, before the meeting starts. It is so obvious yet technology problems occur far too regularly. Technology time-wasters.

Before the meeting begins, the chair needs to visit the space where the meeting is to be held and decide where he or she is going to sit. The meeting room and its layout should not come as a surprise if you are chairing the meeting. Check it out beforehand. Take the time. Prepare.

The chair should choose to sit at the centre point of the table, with his or her back to any available south-facing window (north-facing in the southern hemisphere, e.g. Australia). The chair should be able, and willing, to command the space – and from time to time surprise people.

Table shapes

The ideal table for chairing is oval. This is the table shape that Thomas Jefferson chose for The Rotunda he designed at the University of Virginia in Charlottesville, completed in 1826.

But many meetings use long, thin tables which can cause people to be too far away from the chair, with audibility becoming a problem as a result. A civil servant told me that in 10 Downing Street, the table used by the Cabinet, chaired by the British Prime Minister, "is coffin-shaped. Everyone can see everyone."

If you as chair sit in the middle of a long, thin table, it is not easy to see people on either side of you to left and right. Seeing people and their body language is important. More reticent, less experienced members of meetings, whose wisdom may be in inverse relationship to their quantity of words and willingness to offer them, do not necessarily indicate they want to speak but their body language can indicate that is the case. Bringing out the more reticent members of meetings, getting them to speak and offer views, is a theme that runs through the whole of this book.

In the dining room at the National Trust's Coughton Court near Shakespeare's Stratford-upon-Avon, an historic long, thin table can be seen. It is five metres long and one metre wide, formed of one single board of solid oak, resting on a frame. At the end of a meal, the board was lifted up and turned over, allowing the underside to be used at the next meal (having been presumably licked clean by the dogs). From this historic refectory table design come the words 'board table', 'board of directors', 'board chair' (and the expression 'turning the tables').

Those who do not like long, thin tables and have no access to oval or round tables often use modular tables Their great advantage is that they can be made smaller or larger depending upon meeting numbers and the sizes of meeting rooms. They are best arranged in a U-shape with the chair and secretariat at the bottom of the U, members on two sides and the screen across the top of the U. I personally find the gap between modular tables can push people apart and can reduce audibility in some rooms. The single table surface with people across from each other on both sides brings people together more. *Meetings are about bringing people together – in every sense.*

Audibility

Audibility is key to successful meetings. It is very important that each person can hear every other person clearly. Choosing the right room for meetings obviously affects audibility. In many meetings the acoustics of the architecture are not very good, and some people have a tendency to mumble, looking down into their papers or their tablets and smartphones. The chair should feel no embarrassment in asking participants to look up and speak up and/or to ask people (in the larger meeting) whether they can hear properly. It is a matter of keeping the chin up and projecting the voice which everyone can do, if gently reminded to do so.

At a recent university meeting cum seminar the illustrious chair had obviously not thought about audibility for himself or other main speakers, so interested and engrossed was he in the topic of discussion. There were no mikes (it was quite a big room, long and thin) and people at the back were really struggling, especially to understand those who were not native English speakers. When you are chairing, imagine you are sitting in the back-most row and ask and ensure at the start of meetings whether the people there can hear the proceedings. If there are audibility concerns, then ensure mikes are in place (and that they work!).

Microphones

Managing microphones to ensure audibility for larger meetings is part of the chair's art. I personally find hand-held mikes a bit clumsy and would urge the use, where possible, of neck mikes or fixed mikes on stands, on the rostrum. Don't believe the oft-heard cry that this room does not need mikes – it usually does. Hand-held mikes reduce the chances of audibility if they are not held correctly (not easy even for pros). They also stop people having two hands free (when they are using notes or speeches that are written out).

In conferences it is a good idea to get your speakers to take time to talk to the audio-visual technician about how to use the mikes. It is easy to stand at the rostrum and be too close to the fixed mike, causing irritating bumping. And it is easy to turn left or right away from the fixed mike at the rostrum in order to look at the screen or talk to a fellow panellist, and go off mike without knowing it.

Audio and video conferencing BC (Before Covid)

It is worth having rules about audio conferencing such as no phoning in from noisy spaces (the nearby coffee shop); and those meeting in real life (IRL) being required to speak up. IRL is an apt expression that a colleague uses in her contributions to Chapter 9 on virtual chairing.

It is frustrating to phone in to a meeting via audio conference and find oneself unable to hear half of what is being said in the physical meeting room. Also, it is easy for the chair to forget the invisible people phoning in to the audio conference and just pay attention to those physically in the room sitting IRL with the chair. Those phoning in rightly get upset. Thank them especially at the end of meetings (if they have not already silently dematerialised).

Traditional-style video conferencing is usually better than audio conferencing (but historically much more expensive). Well designed, it can ape a normal physical meeting fairly exactly. Board members need to remember they are on camera. Nose-picking spotted at the other end of a video conference Board meeting I was chairing caused juvenile amusement at my end, which had to be quelled.

But audio and video conferencing, having been a side show in physical meetings over many years, and a useful adjunct to the traditional physical meeting, have now come centre stage.

In 2020, with the Covid pandemic striking the world, new-style audio and video conferencing platforms such as Zoom and Microsoft Teams came to prominence. They have become the drivers of meetings – virtual as distinct from physical meetings. Meetings running over low-cost broadband networks, not high-cost phone and video circuits. The last chapter of the book looks at chairing in a virtual world, and the lessons being learnt from virtual chairing amidst a plethora of new meeting technologies/platforms.

However, whether chairing meetings physically or virtually, it seems that the concerns of the chair appear to remain remarkably consistent. Such as audibility!

PREPARING TO CHAIR – MEETING DISCIPLINE

In addition to clarity about strategic and technical matters, the chair needs also to be clear about meeting discipline.

Introductions

At the start of the meeting ensure that all participants know each other and are introduced or introduce themselves – name and, where appropriate, role. It does take a bit of time but it is worth it. It is even more important in virtual meetings. Don't assume that everyone knows everyone else – there is always likely to be a newcomer in the room. If you have an outside visitor to speak at your meeting, introductions round the table are courteous.

The chair should try and know and remember everyone's name, but this is not easy with bigger meetings. The London-based Broadband Stakeholder Group (BSG), which I chaired until recently, has anything up to 20 members attending, often with new faces. BSG colleagues kindly put a hand-written table plan in front of me showing who was sitting where, and updated it as stragglers arrived. As chair you are expected to know the names of people attending the meeting so that you can call them to speak – easy with small meetings, difficult with large; easy when young, more difficult with age!

Meeting purpose

Having done introductions, state clearly what the purpose of the meeting is, how long it is expected to run and what the outcomes ("deliverables" in the jargon) are planned to be. Having a clock on the wall, ideally opposite the chair, helps to remind people of the English poet Andrew Marvell's "Time's wing-èd chariot".[2] The chair of a meeting always needs to keep up the momentum of the meeting, so that it neither drags nor feels rushed. It is not always easy to maintain a balance, especially if the issues are complex. A good chair injects energy into meetings. There are lean-back chairs leading from behind and emitting less obvious energy and lean-in chairs leading from the front and emitting more energy into the room. Both can work well and I look at these contrasting styles in Chapter 4.

Punctuality

Meetings should start on time. Punctuality demonstrates discipline and reminds us all of good order – sensible values for any organisation. Sloppiness with punctuality can quickly degenerate into general organisational sloppiness. I have been accused as chair of keeping my watch three minutes fast. Giorgio Armani: "Eighty per cent of what I do is discipline. The rest is creativity".[3]

Waiting ten minutes for one person to arrive is not an efficient use of time. I tend to start on time and close the door, thus embarrassing latecomers a little. There are always exceptions to rules – the VIP has to be waited for, however long she or he takes to arrive. A latecomer, who seems to be becoming a regular latecomer, may need to be gently reminded in private outside the meeting that his or her time is probably not more important than the time of the people in the room who have been punctual and had to wait. A good example of the loss of productivity from meetings that Simon Jenkins highlighted in the *Guardian*. Not to mention hope!

Ownership

A key job of the chair in meetings is to encourage ownership of the ideas being discussed and the decisions being taken. When people feel that they have ownership of something, in any walk of life, they are more involved, more effective and things work better. Some chairs find it difficult to delegate ownership (or success) – although they may be very quick to delegate failure. Not to mention politicians.

Thinking strategically about meetings you chair, double-checking technical issues ahead of time, keeping sensible discipline and sharing/delegating ownership of decisions and actions will reduce the opportunity cost of meetings small and large. The next chapter looks at chairing small meetings.

REFERENCES

1.   Northcote Parkinson, C. (1986), *Parkinson's Law*, London: Penguin Books Ltd.
2.   Marvell, A. (1681), *To His Coy Mistress,* www.poetryfoundation.org.
3.   Armani, G. (2014), *Touring Exhibition – The Glamour of Italian Fashion 1945–2014*, London: Victoria & Albert Museum.

CHAIRING SMALL MEETINGS

This small chapter looks at the issues that may arise when chairing small meetings. Paradoxically perhaps, chairing small meetings can be more difficult than chairing larger meetings.

This chapter defines small meetings in two different ways: 1) small in the sense of family meetings, clubs, management meetings of apartment owners, parents running the local playgroup; 2) small in the sense of the small number of people attending the meeting in any environment – from large corporate to small private.

Chairs in this chapter are also defined in two ways – those who are more experienced at chairing and those who are new to it or less experienced.

SMALL MEETINGS WITHIN THE LARGER ORGANISATION

Curiously perhaps, I find that small meetings of three or four people – both within the corporate/private sector environment or the larger public sector organisational environment – can quickly have three or four chairs. If the three or four know each other then there is less formality, and less need for chairing except for the occasional touch on the tiller. These small meetings are often taken on the run, with no meeting rooms booked in advance. There is less distraction in a smaller meeting. Audibility and table shapes are unlikely to be a problem. Members are less likely to be seen looking at their screens to check emails or news, something they may do in larger meetings without being noticed. The chair does not have much if any downtime. There is greater concentration, I find, and a greater pressure to get on with it and finish as soon as possible. This suits the lean-in chairing style outlined in Chapter 4 – as distinct from lean-back.

The chair probably does not have any secretariat at the meeting to help with administration. But there will probably be less bureaucracy anyway and no time or desire for formal agendas and papers.

The chair should be aware of members who are more outspoken at the smaller meeting but who do not want their remarks relayed to a wider public afterwards. Consider a gentle application of the Chatham House Rule (Chapter 8). According to the Rule, the content and ideas can be used but without any attribution to named people. The small meeting may be judged to be beyond the Chatham House Rule and therefore fully "private and confidential". In this case the content and ideas cannot be used.

RECORDING TECHNOLOGY

A feature of the modern digital world is the existence of recording technology which is readily available, unobtrusive and easy to use, from smart phones to the Zoom virtual chairing platform. At the Annual General Meeting of a professional association of academics, consultants and policy-makers, conducted on Zoom and described in more detail in Chapter 9, I noticed halfway through that the red light on my screen indicated that the meeting was being recorded. I was not aware of this. When meetings are being recorded, people will tend to take greater caution. The chair should make it clear to members at the start of the meeting, physical or virtual, that the meeting is being recorded, and why. Members may not agree and may, after discussion, reverse the decision to record. In the modern world where privacy and personal data have become a central public policy concern for citizens, politicians and technology companies, we are right to be upset when we find we are being recorded without prior knowledge. Chairs are responsible for the status of all meetings they chair. They should make the status clear to all at the start and – if necessary – remind everyone during the proceedings.

The other disadvantage of recording technology is that members of a meeting being recorded are likely to be more cautious, more inhibited, thus not saying what they really mean and what they really think.

I can think of a university meeting where sensitive hidden truths remained hidden as a result. To the detriment of events that followed.

At the end of a smaller meeting, it is important to discuss what has been agreed, whether and how it should or should not be minuted and where it might fit in to any larger meeting that needs to be convened or that might already be looming on the horizon. One can think of small meetings where the last thing that is needed is any sort of record or minute, even if there was time to write them.

SMALL MEETINGS – E.G. FAMILIES, PARENTS, APARTMENT OWNERS – WITH MORE EXPERIENCED CHAIRS

Experienced chairs from, for example, the larger organisational environment have to be careful chairing these "small" meetings. They will almost certainly be welcomed and invited to chair because of their prior experience – with noticeable relief from members who do not feel confident enough to chair.

But more experienced chairs can, if they are not careful, drive too hard and put people off. Members attending a meeting with a more experienced chair do not want to feel they are being steam-rollered (even if, towards the end of the meeting, they are likely to experience being somewhat steam-rollered). Chairs need to be more relaxed and informal whilst keeping some – not too obvious – discipline. Biscuits, tea and coffee are important lubricants. In coffee or tea breaks (*Don't eat into lunch*, Chapter 8), chairs can talk quietly to a member who appears not to be happy with the thread of discussion.

More time needs to be taken by the chair, or a member of the meeting with specialist knowledge, to explain the issues at stake, which may be quite technical in nature. In the larger world of the public or private sector, such technical matters are more likely to be understood by members of the meeting. In the family meeting, for example, the role of lawyers, how wills and inheritance tax work, may not be familiar to all those attending the meeting. The apartment block management company meeting will consider matters such as leasehold, freehold, content and buildings insurance, broadband provision. At most meetings small or large these days, liabilities of one sort or another are not far away. At the annual meeting of apartment owners, smoke alarms, for example, may need to be checked to ensure that they are working in each apartment.

ATTENTION TO DETAIL AND 80:20 THINKING

Attention to detail (like smoke alarms) recurs again and again in this book as an important characteristic of a good chair (and a good Chief Executive Officer (CEO)). The balance between detailed knowledge and broader strategic thinking is not easy to achieve, but should always be aimed at.

Chairs need to be able to judge when 80:20 thinking is sufficient for the specific decision being taken by the meeting. Judgements or decisions can often be made with only an estimated 80 per cent understanding of the topic, given that gaining a detailed understanding of the last 20 per cent is likely to be too costly in time or money. Also understanding the last 20 per cent may not alter the decision or judgement being made anyway. Launching manned space rockets or resolving some family rows will require 100:0 thinking.

SMALL MEETINGS – E.G. FAMILIES, PARENTS, APARTMENT OWNERS – WITH LESS EXPERIENCED CHAIRS

People new to, or less experienced at, chairing may find it useful to seek help before they chair these types of meeting. A friend, relative or colleague can point out key things to think about, much of which was described in Chapter 1. What is the issue to be resolved? That is the heart of the matter. Preparation and clarity are running themes of the chair's life.

Helping a friend who was tasked with chairing a family meeting concerned with agreeing how the parental estate should be distributed, taught me (and her) a lot about handling a difficult small meeting. A very fraught issue, emotions running high, hidden resentments emerging into the light, with the chair trying to retain objectivity. I suggested she had a pre-meeting one-to-one with the potentially most difficult person to reduce the meeting room temperature.

The chair should be clear, before the meeting starts, as to the optimal outcome of the meeting. Chairs of family meetings need to think about the issues long and hard in the days before the meeting, rather than just turn up and try to wing it. Later in the book it is noted that males, much more than females, in my experience, are likely to try and wing it.

It is perfectly sensible for less experienced chairs of small meetings to acknowledge, as the meeting starts, that they are not that used to chairing. This will win sympathy and support that you may need when the going gets tougher later.

Both less and more experienced chairs need to make smaller meetings friendly. The members attending may be friends or relatives, neighbours or parents with children at the same school. But there will be decisions which have to be taken and may be unpopular with one or other member. At this point the meeting becomes more procedural and less friendly. It helps sometimes if the chair is explicit about this change of gear.

Amidst all the friendliness and informality of smaller meetings, the chair has to learn to know when and how to become more formal, so that decisions can be taken. Decisions that have the support of most if not all members of the meeting. Hard decisions can be taken, and summarised clearly by the chair, ideally without losing warmth. Leaving matters vague at the end of a meeting is not normally an optimal strategy.

It helps, when the meeting needs to become more formal, if the chair can retain a degree of objectivity, suppressing his or her special interest in the matter under discussion. At this point, the daughter or the son of the family is the chair of the family meeting, trying to gain consensus. Not the daughter or the son concerned with her or his self-interest. Facilitation, a variation of chairing, discussed in Chapter 8, requires the chair not to take sides, but to be able to explain one side to the other if needed, and continually make sure that everyone in the room knows what the issue under debate is. Chairs of all meetings should have a nose for realising there is some lack of clarity or understanding in the room and then devote time, explicitly, to clarification. We are talking about *this*, we are not talking about *that*. You may want to talk about *that*, but we are all agreed that at this moment we are talking about *this*. One of my favourite chairs was very good, in both large and small meetings, at hauling everyone back to reality, in a friendly but firm way.

At the end of the meeting, there needs to be clarity as to what has been decided. The chair has to press hard for this, avoiding the easier option of leaving matters vague when there is unresolved dissent and disagreement. Written and agreed records, which sound overly formal, will be a good insurance policy against differing memories at a later time. So many of these smaller meetings can be ruined when family members, for example, a few weeks or months later, do not agree what was or was not decided. The ideal decision(s) at the end of smaller meetings are those that have full agreement in the room. If that is not the case, it is important that the minority agree to accept the majority decision and do not try, and are not allowed, to rewrite history in the weeks following the meeting.

CONCLUSION – CHANCE ENCOUNTERS

A smaller meeting of three or four in the corporate world may be called with little notice because of a growing but only partially formulated concern about something. Thus the clarity of the purpose of the meeting in the larger meeting may be missing in the smaller meeting. A small meeting in a large company which had very productive results was once described to me as a "chance encounter".

Chairs and meetings and organisations in both the public and private sectors should be open to chance, to serendipity. Chance/serendipity plays a larger role in our own lives and the lives of our organisations than we are often ready, as rational beings, to admit. Chairs should try and be good at spotting and taking chances. Even when those chances contain risk. Handling the risk probably requires more than 80:20 thinking!

3

CHAIRING COMPANY BOARD MEETINGS – WHAT IS THE BOARD FOR?

A friend asked if I was coming to an event she was organising. I replied I couldn't because of a Board meeting. With a mischievous smile she said, "Is that spelt Board or Bored?" The purpose of this chapter and the next is to try and remove the boredom from Board meetings. There is an issue about paying proper attention to boring stuff however – see later. This chapter and the next try to answer the questions that Board chairs worry about, like how to handle disagreement. But the first and most important question a chair, and Board members, need to be clear about, is …

WHAT IS THE BOARD FOR?

There is one legal provision emanating from the UK's Companies Act 2006[1] that needs to be quoted right upfront in this chapter and be duly engraved on the hearts and minds of all chairs and all Board members of companies, public and private, small and large.

It is central to Board members being absolutely clear for whom and for what Board meetings should be working. Non-executive members of the company Board such as the chair, and executive members of the Board such as the CEO, all share exactly the same role on the Board – that of directors of the company.

Section 172 sets out clearly and comprehensively for all directors their:

Duty to promote the success of the company

(1) A director of a company must act in the way he considers, in good faith, would be most likely to promote the success of the company for the benefit of its members [members = shareholders] as a whole, and in doing so have regard (amongst other matters) to—

(a) the likely consequences of any decision in the long term,
(b) the interests of the company's employees,
(c) the need to foster the company's business relationships with suppliers, customers and others,
(d) the impact of the company's operations on the community and the environment,
(e) the desirability of the company maintaining a reputation for high standards of business conduct, and
(f) the need to act fairly as between members of the company.

WHAT IS THE BOARD FOR? NOT JUST SHAREHOLDERS' INTERESTS

A company's responsibility, and thus the responsibility of all Board members, is not, *repeat not*, just to shareholders' (members') interests. Companies being there just for shareholders is a widely held view which is plain wrong. Under Section 172 1(d) above, for example, a view needs to be taken about such critical environmental issues as global warming/climate change.

SEEKING THE TRUTH

Mentoring a young Board director, I asked him an opening question – "What is the role of the Board? What is the Board for?" He paused, and then said quietly: "To seek the truth".

A Board has seven major functions where truth needs to be located – strategy, holding the exec to account (feet to the fire), risk, reputation, people, diversity and values.

Above all the Board should discourage the kind of culture where senior management only wants to hear the good news. There can be "a cultural disinclination to communicate bad news to their bosses", wrote Andrew Hill in the *Financial Times*.[2] Most of us have served senior managers at one time or another whose vanity precluded the mention of, or exposure to, any bad news.

EVIDENCE-BASED DECISION-MAKING

Seeking the truth encourages Boards to focus on good evidence and, where relevant, good research on which to base their decisions. This helps with the hunt for objectivity. I have had the good fortune to chair a regulator (the UK Radio Authority regulating commercial radio) and be founding deputy chair of Ofcom and chair of its Content Board. Ofcom brought together five regulators in 2002/2003 as the technology, media and telecommunications sectors converged. Ofcom regulates telecommunications, broadcasting and spectrum allocation – and more recently postal services.

It was on those regulatory Boards that the power of evidence-based decision-making really resonated and taught me as a chair to give it central importance. This sounds obvious but evidence can easily be: not sought, neglected, misunderstood, misused or hidden away.

Chairs and Board members of companies, of regulators and, indeed, chairs and members of meetings in any walk of life should be encouraged to seek evidence and scrutinise/challenge it properly. It should become second nature to ask, faced with a decision: What is the evidence? What may be the case for and the case against a particular course of action? And, as emphasized in Chapter 5 on diversity, evidence needs to be sought from a broad base of people, not just narrowly from the usual suspects.

The Ofcom Content Board regulates six issues that arise with broadcast content in the UK across television and radio (not the Internet). Is the content of the programme *accurate* and politically *impartial*? Could the content cause *harm* or *offence*? Does the content breach individuals' *privacy* and/or is it *fair* to an individual? In my role as chair, it was crucial to probe all sides of a complaint – the evidence of the complainer(s), the evidence of the broadcaster, listen to or watch the complained-about programme, probe the current perceptions of community standards with regard to what might be considered to cause offence, for example. An Australian content regulator taught me early on that it was often as much *context* regulation as *content* regulation. Swear words being used at 10.00am in a children's television programme are likely to be unacceptable to the broadcasting code of conduct but those very same swear words, in a different context, at 9.30pm at night in adult programming, are likely to be code-compliant. Context is an important part of the facts of the case, an important part of the evidence. Think of difficult human resources (HR) cases in the company, for example – especially ones that surface at the Board. Seek to understand and probe the context before rushing to judgement. Be objective.

DECISION-TAKING

One of the earliest pieces of advice I got in my corporate life was about *when* to take a decision. If you are at point A on a timescale stretching to point M, when you Must take the decision, do not take it before about point K or point L. If you take the decision prematurely, before point K, you lose the additional information and advice that could possibly come in to help you make a better decision. This is not an argument for indecisiveness, but for taking decisions when you have to – and not before. Being satisfied or not with 80:20 thinking, as described in Chapter 2, is an important part of the decision-taking journey from A to K, L, M.

CREATURES OF STATUTE

Regulators like Ofcom and the Radio Authority are "creatures of statute". Whilst companies have to consider general and company law such as Section 172, Ofcom has the 590-page Communications Act 2003.[3] Ofcom Board members are there "to further the interests of consumers in relevant markets, where appropriate by promoting competition". Lord David *Chariots of Fire* Puttnam ensured, during the House of Lords approval of the Act, that the word, and role of, "citizens" should be inserted before "consumers" – Ofcom is there to "to further the interests of citizens in relation to communications matters".

Regulators up to that time had not had to think so directly about broader issues such as citizenship and what actually differentiates a citizen from a consumer. A consumer climbs into a car and drives a few miles to a large supermarket with good parking and low prices. A citizen, by comparison, walks into the local high street, buys food from a number of shops at somewhat higher prices and carries it home. This need to think about citizenship is close to the community and environmental obligations of a company director under Section 172 – obligations not just to shareholders.

WHAT IS THE BOARD FOR? STRATEGY

The executive should propose strategy to the Board – for the Board to agree, disagree, amend, seek more evidence, send back for further work with some suggested courses of action.

However, strategy can so easily be pushed to one side whilst fires are fought and more mundane concerns are ventilated. This takes us back to C. Northcote Parkinson. According to his "law of triviality", a committee spends more time on the bicycle shed which members can understand than on the atomic reactor which members struggle with: "The time spent on any item of the agenda will be in inverse proportion to the sum [of money] involved".[4]

Annual strategy meetings should be organised when time can really be given to strategy, proper time. If held away from the office, with an overnight, they can also encourage bonding. Bonding yields trust and trust yields truth. I do not apologise for repeating key obsessions of mine as a chair. Truth. Trust. Teamwork. The basics.

But the area of strategy can generate more bullshit on a Board than anything else, with grand-sounding words and grand-sounding visions. Keep it simple.

REPORT WRITING

I have chaired two independent reviews for the British Government – one on the future of Royal Mail commissioned by a Labour Government and one on copyright licensing in the digital age commissioned by a Conservative Government. The review process taught me three things about writing reports, which are especially relevant to company Boards and writing/approving strategy papers.

Beware bullet points

Writing stuff down in sentences with main verbs may sound rather old-fashioned. But the process helps clarify what people really mean, especially when discussing and agreeing strategy. You may not know what your Board members *really* mean until someone starts to write it down. "Oh, I didn't mean *that*" rings out. PowerPoint bullet points, without main verbs, are quick to create, can look impressive but, in fact, can on occasion obfuscate the debate. Writing sentences down ensures that the logic and flow of the argument is forced into the open.

Reports take longer to write than you think

One of the best pieces of advice I received from an experienced chair of Government reviews was: "You can never start writing the final report early enough. Do not leave it until it is too late." My Royal Mail report took me, my panel and team of civil servants four months to write. One of the best Board strategy documents I was involved in took longer than this to finalise – to everyone's surprise. But it became the bible for much of the work and many of the good decisions that followed. It also proved to be a valuable document when the company entered merger discussions. Valuable in the sense of the finally agreed share price!

BE CLEAR ABOUT DIAGNOSIS BEFORE MOVING TO SOLUTIONS

This idea came to me from Prime Minister Gordon Brown during the Royal Mail review. He suggested splitting the report of the review into two. The first report, published earlier in the process, sets out the problem/the diagnosis. Later in time, the second and final report sets out solutions. If the diagnosis and solutions are all in one report published together at the same time, people tend not to read the diagnosis and go straight for those solutions which they disagree with.

On company Boards it is very helpful to focus first on what the problem is. Pause. Agree what the problem is. Then and then only, move on to solutions. Agreement on what exactly is the problem can take much longer than envisaged. A good diagnosis makes solution-finding quicker and makes solutions more resilient. Gaining agreement on the diagnosis first also helps to build the consensus around, and ownership of, the solution(s) arrived at later.

WHAT IS THE BOARD FOR? HOLDING THE EXECUTIVE TO ACCOUNT

Holding the executive to account is a key role of a Board. But it is made difficult by a fundamental problem with all Boards – the asymmetry of information. The executive will always know more about the company given they spend every working day in it, compared with the non-execs spending 20–30 days a year. There is no answer to this except requiring the executive to provide on a regular basis good management data that is transparent and consistent and truthful, and non-execs to regularly challenge that data (and visit, if possible, company sites outside Board meetings and talk one to one with executives just below Board level).

The format of data should be consistent month to month, and financial year to financial year, so that there is proper comparability. Boards where the executive, intentionally or unintentionally, changes reporting formats, make it more difficult for the part-time members to separate out fact from fiction and undertake true comparisons of performance, time period to time period. During the previous financial year EBITDA (earnings before interest, tax, depreciation and amortisation) was measured but from the new financial year the plan is to measure EBIT (earnings before interest and tax). Depreciation measures how the value in the balance sheet of a physical, tangible asset, for example the IT system, has declined over time since its acquisition and more modern systems have come available. Amortisation spreads the cost of an intangible asset, intellectual property such as patents and trademarks, over the life of that asset.

Faced with the asymmetry of information, non-execs should, I suggest, focus on a detail, in one sense any detail: What does that line in the monthly accounts on page 41 mean? If the answer is evasive or incomprehensible or inconsistent, then it is worth enlarging the field of enquiry around that point. If the answer is clear, then move on.

There is another dimension to the asymmetry of information – too much information. Executives can keep greater control if they bombard the Board with too many, too long, too complex Board papers. Wordiness and long-windedness are the enemy of successful Board meetings.

WHAT IS THE BOARD FOR? WORRYING ABOUT RISK

When I started on sitting on Boards, I cannot remember words like 'risk' surfacing. But in the last 30 years there has been a massive increase in scrutiny of risk. Risk committees, internal audits, heads of risk, risk registers, risk appetites. Much of this has been driven by corporate implosions, Enron, Northern Rock, HBOS, RBS. Did Northern Rock have a risk register? Was the sudden turning off of liquidity/borrowing, which, it is claimed, destroyed Northern Rock, an identified risk?

The risk register is the key. Do people know the organisation's top three risks, and do they make sense? Do the risks change over time? Does the register include, or omit, the concerns that cause worry in reality? The register should inform strategic conversations.

The real risks are usually the "unknown unknowns" in Donald Rumsfeld's memorable phrase, as distinct from the "known unknowns". Covid appears to have been an unknown unknown for many governments and probably should have been a known unknown. The unknown unknowns are probably not on the Board's too infrequently discussed risk register – when the lightning strikes.

Machiavelli in 1532 had the classic insight into risk when he wrote:

> All wise princes consider not only present but also future discords … for being foreseen, they can be easily remedied. … hectic fevers at their beginning are easy to cure but difficult to recognise, but in course of time when they have not at first been recognised and treated, become easy to recognise and difficult to cure.[5]

Today the "known knowns" include such difficult and risky matters as cyber security, with the exposure to risk heightened by virtual meeting technology. *The Economist*:

> Most recently [in 2020] Tom Anthony, a web-security expert, reported that he had discovered a vulnerability in the Zoom web client that would allow a malicious actor to crack the passcode for a private meeting … any private meeting over the last eight months has been vulnerable to eavesdropping, including sensitive internal company discussions and even government cabinet meetings.[6]

Risk, unfortunately, is also boring. The danger is that a Board and Board members spend more time and attention on stuff that is exciting (the latest sale to the USA with the prospect of a Board meeting in New York) and less time on the stuff that is less exciting such as depreciation and amortisation. However, in the boring may lurk the dangers that could threaten the survival of the company – or the opportunities for greater success.

MORE A MATTER OF MARGINAL GAINS THAN SILVER BULLETS

One of the secrets of Norwegian Roald Amundsen's success in reaching the South Pole in advance of Captain Scott in 1911 was his attention to boring detail. "If we are to win, not a trouser button must be missing."[7]

A century later British cycling under the leadership of Dave Brailsford focused on a whole list of (boring?) incremental, marginal gains to improve cycling performance, leading to a glut of Olympic gold medals for Britain. There is seldom just one silver bullet that solves a problem.

Boards can also get complacent, especially when things are going well. In Brian Law's book about a leading family during the Industrial Revolution in nineteenth-century Lancashire, *The Fieldens of Todmorden*, there is a telling quote: "Great profit has a tendency to produce a relaxation of exertion".[8]

WHAT IS THE BOARD FOR? HANDLING REPUTATION

In the modern digital 24-hour news world, a Board has no alternative but to look to the company's reputation, its public relations (PR). It is easy for time not to be spent on this until, suddenly, there is a PR crisis, by which time it may be too late.

The viral impact of modern social media both in terms of speed, negativity and aggression cannot be underestimated. *BBC News* reports that social media "algorithms can go seriously wrong .... Extreme content simply does better than nuance on social media. And algorithms know that."[9]

The edifice of traditional PR is being shaken at its roots. Reputation requires attention.

This is not a modern issue. Two thousand years ago Virgil wrote:

> Of all the ills there are, Rumour is the swiftest. She thrives on movement and gathers strength as she goes ... a huge and horrible monster ... holding fast to her lies and distortions as often as she tells the truth.[10]

The Board cannot worry enough about reputation given the sheer speed and impact of social media. The Board needs to be absolutely scrupulous about anything that could damage reputation, for example poorly managed conflicts of interest and the poorly managed "independence" of non-exec directors (see Chapter 4). Those handling the company's PR cannot be just reactive, which probably worked most of the time in the old world of print and broadcasting. Being proactive towards social media attacks – such is their speed and destructiveness – may not help either and may not be possible. There would appear to be no easy answers other than good, experienced and creative PR people and eternal vigilance by all, on the Board and throughout the company.

WHAT IS THE BOARD FOR? GETTING PEOPLE, DIVERSITY AND VALUES RIGHT

Of all the things a Board needs to aim for and try to get right, the three most important are: *people*, *diversity* and *values*. Over years of

Board experience in companies of many shapes and sizes, private and public, as a member, adviser or chair, almost all the problems that needed to be dealt with, stemmed not from mistakes of strategy and execution but from having the wrong people around the table. The chair should above all be responsible for getting the right people – executives and non-executives – around the table. And indeed the Board members are responsible for ejecting the chair when that person is not right. I asked the CEO of a company why I was needed to join the Board. His sharp response: "To get rid of the chairman".

"Right" means many things and will mean different things to different people with different leadership and chairing styles. "Right" for me stems from my belief that chairing is fundamentally about promoting teamwork and collaboration. "The right people" for me ideally means having as many of the following attributes as possible: skilled and efficient, from diverse backgrounds and experience, intelligent, hard-working, collegiate, trusting and trustworthy and transparent, willing to take tough and difficult decisions not just indulge in soft consensus; good communicator, open to challenge yet challenging, as interested in execution (doing stuff) (finishing) as in strategising (thinking stuff) (vision); combining strategy on the big scale with attention to detail on the small scale; non-hierarchical, devolving power and delegating; lacking in ego – and ideally having a sense of humour and, if possible, personal warmth.

The best CEO I ever had was able to operate at 35,000 feet one minute and be found checking the specifications for new changing rooms in the basement the next. CEOs can and do get lost at 35,000 feet never coming down to earth, or can get lost in the detail and never rise above it. Again, balance. A good chair should also seek this balance between attention to detail on the one hand and big strategic overview on the other. As should all Board members.

The best chair I served under was able to achieve another sort of balance – operate in the most collegiate way, as a team member, and at the same time balance this with an ability to keep a certain distance, a certain loftiness. This is especially necessary when tough decisions arise about getting rid of the "wrong" people – for example other non-execs. We all have to fight the desire to be loved.

As chair, do you have around the table the right people, whatever right means in your situation? The right execs and the right non-execs? That is the question you should ask on a regular basis and the Board should ask. With regard to the execs, if it turns out that the Chief Financial Officer (CFO) or the CEO is not the right person for the job, then do not give him or her too much benefit of the doubt. Remember Machiavelli's sound advice about illnesses being easy to cure when difficult to diagnose, and difficult to cure when easy to diagnose. The "not right" person or persons must go. Get on with it. They must be replaced, however painful (and risky) that can be. I myself have given people the benefit of the doubt. Instead of them departing, they have stayed around spreading gentle poison. Their exit six months later is that much more damaging and much more painful.

This is also true of collaboration and joint ventures. Some years ago, a collaboration with another company was not going well. Instead of ending the collaboration (which the CEO wanted) and facing some awkward consequences, I and the Board agreed to carry on. That was a mistake.

SKILL SETS

The chair needs to think about what skills he or she wants around the table. For non-execs, I favour those who have a good forensic, vertical knowledge of the sector or sectors in which the company is operating – be it retail, banking, creative industries, telecoms, education, manufacturing. For the audit and remuneration committees, members are needed with good horizontal skills – i.e. accounting and HR. See Chapter 6.

I undertook a Board evaluation for a chair who was concerned that her Board had too many people on it. The agreed aspiration was to reduce the numbers to 11/12. Asking each Board member in one to ones what skills were needed on the Board and where they themselves fitted in to that skills inventory (or not), was uneasy-making but effective. Some members just elected to exit.

"The right people" means above all a true diversity of people, reflecting a multicultural society and world, and a true diversity of viewpoints. I return to this subject in Chapter 5.

REFERENCES

1. *Companies Act 2006* (2006), London: The Stationery Office Ltd.
2. Hill, A. (10 December 2018), *Financial Times*.
3. *Communications Act 2003* (2003), London: The Stationery Office Ltd.
4. Northcote Parkinson, C. (1986), *Parkinson's Law*, London: Penguin Books Ltd.
5. Machiavelli, N. (2011), *The Prince*, London: Penguin Classics.
6. *The Economist* (18 August 2020), economist.com.
7. Huntford, R. (2002), *Scott and Amundsen*, London: Abacus.
8. Law, B.R. (1995), *The Fieldens of Todmorden*, London; G. Kelsall.
9. Clayton, J. and Kleinman, Z. (17 August 2020), *BBC News*, online.
10. Virgil (1991), *The Aeneid*, translated by David West, London: Penguin Classics.

4

CHAIRING BOARD MEETINGS – HOW TO GO ABOUT IT

Getting people, diversity and values right is a key aim of the chair and of the Board. Perhaps paradoxically, getting people, diversity and values right is also the key way of achieving the Board's other aims and functions.

Having clarity as to what a Board and Board meetings are for, how does the chair go about delivering the required outcomes? What is the process of chairing? What is your style?

CHAIRING STYLES

There are two contrasting chairing styles, briefly mentioned in Chapter 1. Lean-in and lean-back. Lean-back chairs do indeed lean back, intervene rarely, direct less often and let the meeting run itself as much as possible. This can be perfectly effective in my view if the meeting is relatively small and if the Board members are bright, alert, on the front foot, have read the papers, know their stuff and know each other well. Lean-back chairing is sometimes referred to more generally as leadership from behind.

I am a preternaturally lean-in chair. Two of the best chairs I have served under were preternaturally lean-back. A lean-in chair intervenes more often, feeling it important to inject energy and direction into a Board meeting to stop it wandering. If there are shy, more reticent, less experienced Board members, a lean-in chairing style may bring them out.

When members of the Board start saying the same things twice, it is time for either type of chair to lean in and lend some direction. You can try both styles but most of us are one or the other by personality and inclination. The lean-in chair can annoy members if he or she pushes too hard. The lean-back chair can annoy if she or he does not push hard enough and meetings go on longer than is really necessary. Meetings are probably shorter with lean-in chairs. I can think of one excellent lean-back chair who got so interested in the topics under discussion that he often lost track of time and even, more than once, his place in the agenda. A dutiful deputy chair or senior independent director can gently nudge the chair back on track.

As chair, the choice of deputy chair (or senior independent director as the deputy is often called) can make the difference between your success and your failure. Someone who can chair well in your absence, who has complementary strengths and someone you can trust implicitly. Someone who can, on an annual basis, discuss with the other non-executives your performance and then quietly suggest where you might be able to perform better. Appraisals and performance improvement are not just for executives in the company. As chair, don't be bruised if colleagues point out things you could do better.

BOARD SIZE

Size of Board affects chairing style but can be contentious, irrespective of chairing style.

Some people are content with 16–20 Board members plus a few senior executive staff in attendance. One argument for the large Board is about not upsetting people – which is a poor argument in my view and plays to soft consensus – a bad thing. Overly large Boards can change the style, and possibly effectiveness, of the meeting itself.

I asked the chair of a large public sector organisation for whom I was doing a Board evaluation, what he wanted in a Board meeting. He said "A conversation". Ironically his Board had some 20 members plus executive staff – I once counted 30 people in the room for a Board meeting. He agreed that there was seldom if ever a conversation. He found himself instead, in response to hands raised, calling out "I will take Bob, then Mary, then Philip". And of course Bob then Mary then Philip are likely to be responding, somewhat randomly, to different points made earlier, and are likely to be making mini speeches and not responding to what each other has just said. Not a conversation more a recital.

An experienced chair and Board member has suggested to me that a very large Board helps concentrate power more easily in the chair or CEO. Something I believe to be undesirable. A smaller Board can hold both chair and CEO more effectively to account.

I would argue that keeping a Board to 10–12 maximum is more likely to achieve a conversation at Board meetings. Be wary of allowing executive staff who are not Board members to attend (except when invited as visitors to speak about, or discuss, specific agenda items). The presence of non-Board member executive staff at Board meetings often starts without anyone noticing and can become a (bad) habit. It increases the number of people in the meeting. But more importantly, it can favour those non-Board member execs who are present over those who are not present, thus causing tensions below Board level. Also Board member non-execs are likely to be wary of talking openly about staff issues if non-Board staff are present. I was half-way through a rather questioning view of one member of staff when I realised that a good friend was sitting in on the Board meeting, somewhat hidden in the second row. Board directors should feel free to talk at Board meetings about difficult and sensitive matters and not be constrained by non-Board member executive staff present.

THE DIFFERENCE BETWEEN EXECS AND NON-EXECS

The chair needs to be clear about the difference between non-executive members of the Board (the chair in the UK is usually himself or herself non-executive), executive members of the Board and executives below Board level.

The difference in roles between execs and non-execs is quite simple:

- Execs tell people in the company what to do.
- Non-execs do not tell people in the company what to do.

Non-execs on Boards often come from a strong executive background and thus find it very difficult not to be executive and not to start telling people what to do. They are not used to being in an advisory role. This requires a lot of effort to put into practice. Sitting on one's hands is not easy in the early days of being a non-exec.

A good non-exec is a good adviser, a consigliere.

If the executive in the end is not up to it, change the executive and don't attempt to become the executive. There may of course be a crisis when non-executives have to run the company for a short period. But that is the exception not the rule.

Changing one or more of the executives is the most important part of the non-execs' power. But succession planning on Boards never gets the attention it deserves. Because it is embarrassing.

Succession planning, in relation to both non-executive and executive Board members, should be on the Board agenda at least once a year, if not more often. The Financial Reporting Council's (FRC's) *UK Corporate Governance Code* helps by requiring non-executive directors or chairs to be on a Board for not more than nine years in normal circumstances.[1]

Executives just below Board level and not Board members are sometimes called, perhaps unfortunately, the marzipan layer. I recommend chairs and other non-execs spending real time outside Board meetings, when possible, talking with executives in the so-called "marzipan layer". These executives close to, but not on, the Board, know where the bodies are buried.

CHAIRS AND CEOS – DIFFERENT ROLES

The Economist attributes the fall of mighty General Electric (GE) in the USA to, amongst other things, "America's cult of the chairman-chief executive. When both roles are held by one man (they are mostly men), underlings and boards find it harder to challenge big decisions, even when potentially ruinous."[2]

In the UK, as set out in the FRC's *UK Corporate Governance Code*, the chair of the Board is required to be non-executive and executive chairs are frowned upon. If you as a Board want to breach the *Code*, for example by having an executive chair, you are required to explain your reasons to shareholders. In the USA executive chairs are the norm.

I think it is simple really. The chair runs the Board that governs the company and the CEO runs the company. These are different tasks, requiring different people. This also ensures that not all power is in one pair of hands – power is distributed which I believe to be a good thing for open and accountable governance. The CEO, and indeed the chair, individually or as a pair, can wield non-consultative power – I prefer consultative power. Chapter 5 looks at the importance of consultation, consultation, consultation.

The relationship between the non-exec chair and the CEO should, fairly obviously, never be either too cosy or too far apart. A case of proper balance.

The chair may also need to remind executive directors on the Board from time to time not to confuse their two different roles. They are the managers who run the company and they are directors on the Board responsible for the company's governance. When a manager enters the boardroom for a Board meeting, she or he has to forget the needs, interests and expectations of being a manager. The focus, as a Board director, has to be unequivocally on the best long-term interests of the health of the company and its many stakeholders. Section 172.

CHALLENGE AND SUPPORT

The non-exec chair and the other non-exec Board members need to get the balance right between challenging the executive and supporting them.

Too much challenge leads to demotivated execs. Too much support leads to executive capture. I remember vividly a Board with one non-exec who was so aggressive in challenging the executive, so non-supportive, that the execs offered to resign. Fortunately we managed to engineer the exit of the troublesome non-exec, not the execs. The first meeting after the non-exec went was a delight (and was productive too). The Board settled back within a few minutes into a better rhythm. The chair must keep an eye on the balance between support and challenge and try to get it right most of the time.

I asked a busy CEO what he looked for in a chair. She or he needs to be: "Robust when needed. Good at delivering hard advice in warm tones. Always has one's back."

BOARD PREPARATION, PAPERS AND COMPANY SECRETARIES

Good Boards, whatever the size of company, need a good engine room and a good chief engineer/secretariat. The chief engineer in the shape of the company secretary/general counsel is a key success factor for a Board. She or he is a key guide (and often mentor) for the non-execs, policing and guarding due process. Some non-execs often do not think about the role and importance of the general counsel/company secretary. And Boards can unwisely downplay or diminish their role – especially if the role is performed by females and the Board is predominantly male.

Given the litigiousness of the modern world, it is sensible to pay attention to the company secretary and to the mem and arts (Memorandum and Articles of Association). Has the company secretary secured proper Directors and Officers liability insurance? Are the Board minutes kept in store efficiently year in year out? You never know when what was said and agreed on 26 January 20.. might turn out to be important. Class actions against Boards by unhappy shareholders can take years to unfurl.

The good company secretary brings objectivity to the Board, a sensible neutrality. Especially during periods of great disagreement and upheaval. He or she can be a valuable bridge and translator between execs and non-execs. The company secretary is there to remind the Board of its legal responsibilities, in relation to such obvious issues as not trading whilst insolvent. My favourite company secretary was over six feet tall but somehow was quietly invisible most of the time. When a legal storm broke, unexpectedly, he was right on top of it. And visible.

Good company secretaries will ensure that papers go out in due time ahead of Board meetings, in hard copy for those who want them in that form or posted to the relevant digital drawer. Late arrival of papers is a constant source of annoyance to busy non-execs, increases the asymmetry of information unnecessarily and increases the concern about it. What might the execs be trying to hide?

Papers tabled on the day of the Board can be even more asymmetric and annoying. The chair should in most cases just not allow it. Worse still is Death by PowerPoint – great packs of PowerPoint slides that suddenly emerge from nowhere at the start of a Board meeting, not sent out in advance. In hard copy and on the screen, the endless stream of slides will grind the non-execs into weary submission. Asymmetry of information in spades.

PREPARING FOR BOARD MEETINGS

The chair and company secretary and CEO need to prepare for a Board meeting in advance. Agendas need to be agreed and the chair needs to have a real knowledge of the papers to be presented. The chair should try and insist that the other non-execs follow suit and have read the Board papers.

Mervyn King, author of *The Corporate Citizen: Corporate Governance for All Entities*,[3] kindly reviewed this chapter and wrote to me with some good advice:

> After having a vote on the issue at hand I would ask a director to explain why he or she voted in favour of the proposed resolution. If he or she has not really understood the report or the discussion that has ensued at the meeting, he or she will sit there embarrassed. The consequence, however, is that diligence improves. Directors do their homework and know that I as chair might test their understanding. Without understanding the issues, the director or member of any organisation is not making a contribution because the company has no mind of its own. The individual directors acting as a collective become the mind, soul and conscience of the company. The chair has to direct that collective conscience so that stakeholders see the company as a responsible corporate citizen.

CONFLICTS OF INTEREST

As chair, do take conflicts of interest seriously. Non-exec Board members, especially if they are enjoying portfolio/pluralist careers, can easily overlook where one current client or project or Board membership overlaps another current client or project or Board membership in a detrimental way. Conflicts of interest can damage reputation, both personal and corporate, very quickly indeed. This should be a permanent item at the top of every agenda of meetings in the private sector as well as the public sector – after minutes and matters arising.

It was when I became chair of the regulator, the Radio Authority, that I came to see the real importance of managing conflicts of interest. The chairs of most meetings, not just regulators, need to keep potential conflicts of interest firmly in mind. Problems involving them, especially in public bodies, make front page news very quickly. I had got caught up in a conflict of interest issue when a Board member of the Radio Authority a decade earlier. Despite doing it by the book and following the conflict of interest rules to the letter (and beyond), I still ended up being vilified in the press over a commercial radio licence award.

The answer is to be as transparent as possible. The Radio Authority instituted a public register of members' interests, a public register of gifts and hospitality and public minutes with, for example, only commercially confidential matters redacted.

At a company Board meeting, any change in a Board member's interests since the previous meeting should be reported by the Board member, discussed if necessary and approved (or disapproved!) and then minuted.

Be wary of blind family trusts, where Board members have shareholdings but do not know what those shareholdings are. The media will not understand or care about the nuance, when a conflict of interest involving a shareholding you do not know about explodes.

INDEPENDENCE

There is a related issue to the management of conflicts of interest – independence. The FRC *Code* requires of companies it governs, that: "At least half the board, excluding the chair, should be non-executive directors whom the board considers to be independent".[4] The chair is required to be independent on appointment. Independence means a director not being connected to the company in the past or present in a range of ways, for example an employee of the company within the last five years, or not representing a particular shareholder. As with conflicts of interest, an independent director who turns out to be not independent according to the rules can damage corporate (and personal) reputation.

Independent-mindedness is something that chairs can look for and encourage, especially amongst the non-execs. It is critical to the thinking of regulatory Boards. Prime Minister Thatcher in the 1980s, when privatising energy and telecoms companies, created independent economic regulators of those privatised companies – the idea, called "Thatcherism", that spread around the world. In a Faustian deal, politicians give up control of, and political interference in, those companies, leaving it to the regulator to control them, in accordance with statutes proposed by the Executive (Her Majesty's Government) and approved by the Legislature (the Houses of Parliament).

Regulatory independence has in recent times, in the UK and in other countries, come under pressure when politicians want to take back control, want to override the regulator and reduce, for example, energy prices to the consumer – an obvious vote-winner. Or when politicians want to appoint a chum to a public post (see Chapter 7). Chumocracy replacing democracy.

AGENDAS

There does not need to be great rigidity with agenda formats. Minutes, matters arising (action points from the last meeting), conflicts of interest, CEO report, report of committee chairs – is a normal way to start. The number and length of agenda items that follow should be watched to make sure that the meeting does not overrun. But overrunning is no great sin – as long as it does not become a habit!

Should agendas include suggested times for the various items to be discussed – 0910–0920 etc.? The advantage is that Board members get to know the likely importance of agenda items and time-keeping improves. The disadvantage is that Board members have differing views about the importance of particular agenda items and might feel rushed. As chair, do what feels right for you and the make-up of the Board. If you decide to have timed agendas it is a good idea to try and stick to the times indicated. Separating the agenda into decision papers versus papers for comment/to note can help.

Agendas are a guide to the meeting and are not sacrosanct. I have known chairs disallow a topic from a Board member because it is not on the agenda. There may of course be reasons for disallowing a topic not on the agenda, based on the constitution and rules governing a particular Board. If that is not the case, I normally allow the new discussion. We are seeking the truth. We want to hear from hidden voices.

SEATING PLANS

Where do/should people sit? I am genuinely agnostic on this. There are lots of Board meetings where name plates are set out on the table telling you where to sit, others where you find your own seat, free-seating style. The danger with name plates set out in advance is they may suggest a favoured power structure – who is sat next to the CEO – who is sat next to, or opposite, the chair. But the advantage of name plates is that you can see the names of Board members which you may have forgotten – especially on larger Boards or when there are new members!

Minute: "a brief summary of events or transactions", *Oxford English Dictionary*.[5] I like to have the Minutes secretary next to me or close to me when I am chairing. This is to remind all Board members of the importance of good minutes and the importance of the Minutes secretary who may be quite junior. A second reason for having the Minutes secretary next to or near to the chair is that this allows the chair, at the end of a difficult discussion, to ask if she or he is clear as to what has been decided and what the minutes will say. Proper records of debate and decisions are increasingly important as the requirements of corporate governance tighten upon all of us. After the meeting, the process of approving draft minutes by members is demanding, but crucial. The alleged informality of Prime Minister Tony Blair's Government at the turn of the century acquired the not too flattering description "government by sofa". Those days are gone.

I do not like second rows in meetings if they can be avoided. The second row confers lower status and leads to the meeting being hogged by the first row who are sitting at the table. Second rows also reduce audibility and visibility. Absolutely do not allow your Minutes secretary to sit in any second row.

Try and ensure that "difficult people" do not automatically sit next to each other. Splitting them up reduces conspiratorial side-mutterings. Executives and non-executives should intermingle around the Board table and not sit in separate phalanxes. Side-mutterings should be sat on quickly – the chair should insist on one and only one conversation at any one time around the meeting table. One advantage of virtual meetings (Chapter 9) is that the technology really does not like people speaking over or at the same time as other people in the meeting. But the chat function in virtual platforms like Zoom threatens the "one and only one conversation".

I was evaluating a Board in the media sector and thus was attending their Board meetings. The treatment of visitors to the Board meeting, arriving to present or sit in on specific agenda items, was less than optimal. They had to come in and push around past members seated to find a spare chair. After it was pointed out, the end of the table near the door was reserved for visitors. End of hassle. Beginning of happier visitors. Simple marginal gain.

Finally in relation to seating plans, I prefer to have the CEO or relevant head person opposite me if we are using a single table lay-out. This allows us to communicate non-verbally (the CEO can also indicate someone wishing to speak, whom the chair has not spotted).

DISAGREEMENTS

An important point about chairing meetings, especially Board meetings, relates to the matter of disagreements and conflicts. This can be a matter of personal style. I as chair enjoy disagreements and conflicts because they help establish the truth much more quickly, defining the boundaries of the debate. It is easy for meetings to wander if there is not some clarity as to what is being talked about. Disagreements and conflicts also tell you more about the people around the table, and more quickly. There are other chairs who prefer to take disagreements outside the meeting "off-line".

You will always have disagreement on Boards you chair. Disagreement between non-execs, between non-execs and execs and between execs.

Disagreement between execs is probably the most challenging. Some chairs I have served under will not brook disagreement between execs and certainly will not allow those disagreements to be rehearsed in public at a Board meeting. "Go away and sort it out before you come to the Board", a chair of many years ago said angrily. He was a former naval officer not used to such ill-discipline.

An alternative approach is to invite the disagreement between execs into the Board meeting and ask each side to rehearse their arguments in front of the Board. If the Board is well bonded and trusting of each other, then this can work brilliantly. Otherwise, it may be better to take intra-exec disagreements off-line. But disagreement between execs should not be encouraged to happen too often.

Disagreements between chair and CEO are not to be recommended – at least not during Board meetings. But as a general rule, the airing of disagreements may mitigate risk, may mitigate against the blind spots that any meeting can have and possibly protect against Donald Rumsfeld's "unknown unknowns".

Disagreements can of course degenerate into explosive issues which as chair you are either aware of or, more likely, not aware of – until they explode. If you have your ear to the ground (consultative as opposed to non-consultative), and as a matter of course listen to a range of people not just the Board members, you may be lucky and know of explosive issues ahead of time. They are usually people issues and not matters like strategy. I can remember a Board where the CEO was retiring and the CFO was quite clear that he should take over. This was not a matter for a Board meeting. It ended up, rather sadly, with the CFO himself leaving the company. Off-line, and very explosive (and expensive).

YOUR VIEWS AS CHAIR

Is it the job of a chair to take sides in a meeting? No and Yes.

No. A good chair does not (initially at least) have to disclose his or her position and views. All that this might do is stop voices and views being heard. A chair's job is to try and ensure that meeting attendees have an opportunity to voice their views.

Yes. Ideally, of course, the chair identifies and articulates a view that is the sensible consensus of the people attending and is compatible with his or her own view. Herein lies the real art of chairing – gaining a sensible consensus rather than a lowest common denominator soft consensus.

I asked a civil servant how chairs of Government meetings in Whitehall handle their own views. He told me that when Prime Minister Thatcher chaired meetings, she invariably stated the topic up-front and then gave her view robustly up-front. She thus challenged people to disagree with her. Most chairs would settle for a less fearsome approach, allowing their own view to come out during debate, more organically.

I had one experience of being chaired by Prime Minister Thatcher – a seminar in 10 Downing Street in September 1987 for senior broadcasting executives on broadcasting futures, in the context of the arrival of satellite broadcasting. The Prime Minister was in listening mode, totally on top of the meeting, on top of the agenda and briefing papers (which she appeared not to even glance at). She clearly knew the names and faces of most people present (especially those running television news organisations) and hunted them down during the coffee break. She asked me to open the meeting with a look at the technology. I had brought with me some satellite equipment, and examples of coaxial cable (cable tv), copper wire (telephones) and optic fibre (broadband futures). She had never seen optic fibre before, leaned across and took it into her hand, cradling it there for much of the rest of the seminar. She chaired with an astoundingly detailed knowledge of broadcasting policy, given how much of her time she would normally spend on such a subject. It was at this seminar that she delivered the memorable words to a commercial television executive: "Mr XX, You are the last bastion of restrictive practices!"

AND FINALLY, BACK TO BOARD MEETINGS …

Beware "the bum's rush". It is too easy for the executives to overwhelm the non-execs with a big decision that comes suddenly at them with those masses of PowerPoint slides (probably not seen before the Board meeting) and the urgent need for a decision now, today, this minute. Non-execs should not fall for this. Chairs should not allow it. I cannot think of many decisions that need to be rushed. The Board should clearly not prevaricate but equally should avoid "the bum's rush". They will regret it later in 90 per cent of cases, almost certainly.

One last note in relation to Board meetings. Non-execs should not ever feel embarrassed about having non-exec-only meetings, as the need arises. They are often best placed before or after a normal Board meeting. They are useful for discussing emerging concerns before such concerns are raised with the executive.

REFERENCES

1. Financial Reporting Council (July 2018), *The UK Corporate Governance Code*, London: Financial Reporting Council.
2. *The Economist* (1 August 2020), economist.com.
3. King, M. (2006), *The Corporate Citizen: Corporate Governance for All Entities*, London: Penguin Books.
4. Financial Reporting Council (July 2018), *The UK Corporate Governance Code*, London: Financial Reporting Council.
5. *Oxford English Dictionary* (1933), Oxford: Oxford University Press.

THE RIGHT PEOPLE – DIVERSITY

In any group or meeting, and especially those tasked with governance, there needs to be adequate challenge and proper representation of viewpoints to 'seek the truth'. Everyone around the table should feel comfortable and confident enough to help shape that 'truth', or outcome. A key role of the chair is to ensure that the group is sufficiently diverse to represent a good cross-section of viewpoints and interests. This should be reflected not only in the diversity of viewpoints of the people involved but also in their general approaches to issues and their outlooks (some will be more socially inclusive, some more action-oriented, some more analytical).

The chair's most important task is getting "the right people" around the Board table. If you inherit a Board, this will take time. "The right people" means above all aiming for a true diversity, reflecting a multicultural society and world. A good mix of all genders, younger people, people from different ethnic and social class backgrounds, people with disabilities, people with different sexual preferences. Not just token appointments.

If you are appointing a chair, seek diversity as well. Diversity is a bit like risk. It was not an issue for Boards not that long ago. Boards and chairs were predominantly, dominantly, white and male.

The role of the chair is to invite and encourage healthy challenge. This allows all voices to be heard, and helps the meeting towards a constructive and timely outcome. When addressing issues that affect/reflect large parts of society (citizens as well as consumers), diversity is absolutely essential. With particular issues at stake, greater weight should be given to certain stakeholders, who may not be represented at the meeting.

In Western Australia, as reported by Eliza Borello for *ABC News*, culturally significant aboriginal caves were destroyed by Rio Tinto as a result of their mining activities.[1] Were key stakeholders from the local Pilbara communities involved in Rio Tinto's planning, discussions, meetings and decisions?

A museum designer gives a good example of the need for museum Boards to think about diversity:

> A key issue is to ensure that spaces in museums can be used by a range of different members of the community – age-based, disability/access-related. There is an increasing acknowledgement of the need to welcome visitors from different ethnic backgrounds more effectively, especially since so many UK museum collections were put together during the Victorian 'imperial' age. People who represent these groups and/or have specialist knowledge need to be heard in the planning stages.

Chairing a Board with a member who was blind, made me and other Board members *think* about disability at every meeting. A very real and instructive case of *not* seeing the world as others see it.

DIVERSITY IMPROVES COMPANY PERFORMANCE

The good news is that research consistently demonstrates the benefits of taking diversity seriously. According to the McKinsey report *Delivering through Diversity*, based on research in 2015 and 2018, attention to inclusion and diversity leads to a more effective and successful outcome for the organisation. To quote from this report:

> Many successful companies regard inclusion and diversity (I&D) as a source of competitive advantage, and specifically as a key enabler of growth …. Companies in the top-quartile for gender diversity on executive teams were 21% more likely to outperform on profitability and 27% more likely to have superior value creation. The highest-performing companies on both profitability and diversity had more women in line (i.e., typically revenue-generating) roles than in staff roles on their executive teams.

It's not just gender. Companies in the top-quartile for ethnic/cultural diversity on executive teams were 33% more likely to have industry-leading profitability. That this relationship continues to be strong suggests that inclusion of highly diverse individuals – and the myriad ways in which diversity exists beyond gender (e.g., LGBTQ+, age/generation, international experience) – can be a key differentiator among companies.

The report continues:

There is a penalty for opting out. The penalty for bottom-quartile performance on diversity persists. Overall, companies in the bottom quartile for both gender and ethnic/cultural diversity were 29% less likely to achieve above-average profitability than were all other companies in our data set. In short, not only were they not leading, they were lagging ... more diverse companies are better able to attract top talent; to improve their customer orientation, employee satisfaction, and decision-making; and to secure their license to operate. Designing a truly effective I&D strategy is no small undertaking. But we and the many companies we studied believe the potential benefits of stronger business performance are well worth the effort.[2]

TALENT

Teams where membership and leadership reflect the wider world perform more effectively since issues can be "caught" that might not otherwise be identified. Teams with true diversity will better serve a customer base, for example, when that customer base is itself very diverse. It is my belief, after many years of chairing people, and being chaired alongside people, from playgroup parent organisations to company Boards, that talent is equally shared across people, irrespective of backgrounds and education. So don't waste it. Encourage it. Recruiting for diversity is reinforced in Chapter 7.

A young woman CEO whom I had been mentoring told me:

I have been in countless meetings where I've been asked to take the notes, or pass a message to the receptionist, or change the temperature, or – my all-time favourite – when someone spills a glass I am the person to get the tissues to mop up the mess! … I highly value a chairman that ensures the other Board members take me seriously, even if I don't look/sound like them. On an EU trade body, I was patronised by an old German man … but thankfully the Italian chairman immediately leapt to support my comment and encouraged me to expand. If he hadn't recognised the 'old man patronising the young woman dynamic', I think I may've been intimidated into submission and not spoken for the rest of the meeting!

In today's world, it is unacceptable, dated and insulting to treat anyone like this.

NEW BOARD MEMBERS

The chair needs to be thoughtful when a new Board member arrives, especially when he or she is coming to their first Board, in particular a person coming from a more diverse, less "traditional" background. It is easy to forget, when you have become Board-experienced, the nervousness of that first Board. Where do I sit? What do I say – if anything? What are the key issues of the day? A one-to-one meeting before that first Board between chair and new Board member is sensible. I always agree to requests for one-to-ones with Board members new and old – you never know what they might uncover. And sometimes you may not want to know!

REVERSE DOMINO EFFECTS

With the right people, and with diversity taken seriously and not token-ly, so much else on a Board and in an organisation sorts itself out almost naturally. I call this the reverse domino effect. With the wrong people, nothing sorts itself out and you get the full weight of the domino effect. I think of a consulting assignment to an organisation where there were many things going wrong. We changed the relevant management (one of the many wrong things). Almost immediately after the new management came in, with a much better mix of senior men and senior women, so many of the wrong things seemed to heal themselves. The reverse domino effect. Changing the management was for once a silver bullet.

WALKING RATHER THAN TALKING THE TALK

If you have the right people round the table do they and do you share the same values and are those the values of the company or organisation that is being governed? Are they your values as chair? Talking about values and the "culture" of the company, talking up front about diversity, is worth doing and it is worth then writing down the values, including what is meant by diversity. Thereafter, it is important that Board members display those values in their actual behaviour. In that rather memorable jargon, walk the talk not just talk the talk.

President Reagan's biographer, H.W. Brands, saw one of the President's real talents as being able to say one thing and do something else.[3] That may be good for politicians, but not I believe for Board members. Most of the time.

PAY GAPS

If, as chair, you are serious about gender and ethnic diversity, does the company measure and improve the gender and ethnicity pay gaps, for example?

James Harding, editor of *Tortoise Media*, wrote:

> Prime Minister Theresa May's government opened a consultation on ethnicity pay gap reporting in 2018. It received 300 responses before it closed in January 2019. Since then, nothing.
>
> Gender pay gap reporting has been mandatory for companies with over 250 employees since 2018, and although it was paused in 2020 due to the pandemic, many companies have published this year anyway.
>
> Some big companies have voluntarily published their ethnicity pay gaps for some time, yet opponents to making ethnicity pay gap reporting mandatory often cite issues with data as a key barrier. Even large companies may have small numbers of employees in each of the sub-categories making data comparisons difficult, but lumping everybody into a binary "non-White

British" category isn't acceptable either. Processing and storing information about employees' ethnic identity can itself be legally sensitive.[4]

SELF-CONFIDENCE BUILDING

One of the main issues as chair you need to face up to is self-confidence levels amongst Board members. The traditional male Board member is likely to be self-confident. Too much self-confidence can lead to hubris. The ancient Greeks teach us that hubris can lead to *atë* (folly) and *atë* can lead to nemesis – the implosion of people, companies and organisations.

Female Board members and Board members from less traditional backgrounds may be less self-confident. But a senior executive woman, reviewing this chapter, commented to me:

> Please don't imply that all women or ethnically diverse people lack confidence!! From my experience of being a woman (!), and not a privately educated one at that, those who have gotten this far and are at board/exec level aren't shrinking violets by nature and definitely have a voice – often a strong one. I've met more shrinking violet men in meetings than women – who have tended to be feistier – but also better listeners. By nature of being there, they've most likely had to fight harder to get their way into the room so they sure as hell won't lose the opportunity to speak once they've got there. They might just speak when they actually have something decent to say – unlike their counterpart species who will bellow at any opportunity …!

One Board I chaired had a new young member who was very low in self-confidence, finding himself surrounded by what he described to me as "a bunch of university degrees". This was a first Board and first Board meeting for him. The new member, under the free seating arrangements I liked at the time, sat at the farthest end of the universe. Two years later, encouraged by all those around him, he was sitting confidently almost opposite me, a full and strong member of the Board.

I was mentoring a young British Afro-Caribbean woman re her first Board. Months later, I had seen an advertisement that would have suited her down to the ground. I called her and asked her whether she had applied. She said that she had considered applying and decided not to: "I did not meet all five of the criteria set out in the advert". I looked again at the advert and said to her that most men before applying would have not even looked at the criteria.

More men than women are happy to wing it, in my experience.

Diversity of people around a Board table allows for a richer conversation and a richer choice of who does what, who thinks what. This is just as true if not truer of meetings of organisations beyond the business world. At a meeting about broadband in London, some very disgruntled stakeholders, from diverse backgrounds, were present and did not feel that they had really been listened to. The chair, who was in a hurry, wanted to get through the agenda. A chair must want stakeholders who come with strong viewpoints to attend the meeting and must give them space to contribute. That can be emotional space.

WORDS, WORDS, WORDS

I asked a senior British Afro-Caribbean woman about appropriate language – her response:

> I use the term Black people during Black History Month – to honour Black people's history. Otherwise I use the term "people of colour". There is a strong movement now not to use the term BAME (Black, Asian, Minority Ethnic) as it tends to lump all minorities under one banner and it is not seen as being respectful to the importance of each group's identity. The chair needs to be aware of cultural identity and avoid lumping people from diverse backgrounds together in the belief they represent each other's views and experiences. Everyone has different identities, customs and expectations. Also the values and perceptions they bring to the Board can be wide-ranging.

CONSULTATION, CONSULTATION, CONSULTATION

The biggest lesson I learnt from the two Government reviews that I chaired on the Royal Mail and copyright licensing was the importance of consulting widely. This is at the heart of a chair's translation of the word "diversity" into action. Talk to walk.

You and your team can never consult enough. Forgotten stakeholders do not wish to be forgotten. Less articulate and less visible stakeholders wish to have their voices heard. Outside Board meetings, where possible, visit staff, stakeholders, in their own locations – rather than have them invited to the formal meeting rooms or an empty, rather off-putting Boardroom. Much more can be learnt from them and they are likely to be more truthful and less stiff in their own familiar settings such as their own desk or office or even their home. Don't just rely on submitted written responses to more formal consultations. Those responses seldom tell the real story. They seldom give you "tone". They absolutely don't give you gossip.

At the end of the Royal Mail review, the Communication Workers Union disagreed strongly with one of our three main recommendations – privatisation. But they could not, and did not, say that they had not been fully consulted. They had, encouragingly, fully agreed, earlier in the review process, with our diagnosis of the Royal Mail's problem – lack of modernisation for the digital age.

SLOW PROGRESS WITH DIVERSITY

The previously cited McKinsey Report looked at the progress with action on diversity between 2015 when the original research was undertaken and 2018 when they examined it again:

> [P]rogress has been slow. The 346 companies in our 2015 research (mostly based in the US and UK) have increased average gender representation on their executive teams only 2 percentage points, to 14%, and ethnic and cultural diversity by 1 percentage point, to 13%. What's more, many companies are still uncertain as to how they can most effectively use inclusion & diversity (I&D) to support their growth and value creation goals.[5]

ACTION POINTS

A senior chair, reviewing this chapter, summarised her key advice as follows:

> There has rightly been much attention given to improving diversity at Board level, with the focus being on achieving a more even gender balance. My personal experience is that Boards that are more diverse are more effective and give more rounded advice to the executive. But gender diversity within the Board isn't enough. It needs to translate into and act as a spur for better diversity at exec level, particularly outside roles where the pipeline of women is typically stronger, such as HR. Chairs and Chief Executives have to be really quite determined and apply real creativity and imagination when they recruit – not least as the traditional search firms have less experience of, and weaker networks especially in relation to, ethnic minorities. Looking internationally and even into the public sector can pay dividends.

REFERENCES

1. Borello, E. (11 June 2020), *ABC News, www.abc.net.au.*
2. Hunt, V., Prince, S., Dixon-Fyle, S. and Yee, L. (January 2018), *Delivering through Diversity* McKinsey & Company, Executive Summary.
3. Brands, H.W. (2016), *Reagan: The Life*, New York: Anchor; Reprint Edition.
4. Harding, J. (4 September 2020), *Tortoise Media*, www.tortoisemedia.com.
5. Hunt, V., Prince, S., Dixon-Fyle, S. and Yee, L. (January 2018), *Delivering through Diversity,* McKinsey & Company, Executive Summary.

6

CHAIRING BOARD COMMITTEES AND ANNUAL GENERAL MEETINGS

Given the growing importance of corporate governance, as set out for London-listed companies in the Financial Reporting Council's *UK Corporate Governance Code*,[1] the chairing of Board committees has become more and more important. The chair of the company Board normally only chairs one of the three main Board committees – nominations.

REMUNERATION COMMITTEE – REMCO

Remuneration of senior executives is in the eye of the storm with activist shareholders following the decisions of remuneration committees very closely, and frequently disagreeing with them. Shareholders quite properly want executives to be rewarded in line with their actual performance and want bonuses and long-term incentive plans to be linked to real performance. Chairing remco, the remuneration committee, is thus in the eye of the storm. Executive pay has become hugely political. Another dimension of company reputation easily dented.

As remco chair, you should be clear what the scope of your scrutiny is. At one end, some remcos just concern themselves with the pay and rations of the executive directors and of the non-execs who serve on the Board, with only passing interest in pay and rations below Board level. At the other end, there are remcos which take a much more than passing interest in the pay of the senior management team below Board level and indeed pay rises through the workforce.

But it should be clear that it is the pay of the executives on the Board that attracts the shareholder attention (since for listed companies it will be public information). The remco chair has the delicate task of aiming to get the balance right between under and overpaying. The main reference point is comparability studies with other companies in the same or similar sectors. But these comparability studies, usually undertaken by outside HR consultants, can have the unintended but real consequence of driving up all the pay rates. Especially if every remco decides to pays its executives at rates comparable with companies in the first quartile of company performers. When everyone thinks they should be paid according to the first quartile, pay inflation ignites. I am not sure I have ever served on a Board that did not think itself in the first quartile.

The sensible starting point is for the remco chair to ask the chief executive his or her views on the pay of the executives (including of course the pay of the CEO himself or herself) for the following financial year. Don't leave the process to the dying embers of the current financial year because it always takes longer than you think. The executives should start the trading year knowing what their package is.

Comparability studies will of course be helpful to the negotiations, if not too mechanically followed. But then it comes down to common sense and good judgement. The chair should ensure the she or he is aided and abetted by good remco committee members, carefully chosen for their tough tactfulness, their knowledge of remuneration policy and politics and their real attention to detail.

The corporate heads of HR who run a lot of this process for the CEO and command the data are not to be underestimated. It is therefore useful to have someone on your side working for and with you, the non-execs. On a recent Board remco, we non-exec members hired our own HR consultant. This worked really well and there was some balance of power and some real symmetry of information.

Given that private equity tries to steal executives from the listed sector with much higher potential rewards, clever tax arrangements and no gold fish bowl of visibility, remco has certainly got no option but to pay appropriately. Shareholders do need to be consulted on major changes and can be useful in achieving the right final decisions.

In Board meetings, execs and non-execs work on the same side – most of the time. The fundamental problem of remco is that non-execs very often have to oppose the executive. On the other side of the table.

AUDIT COMMITTEE

Audit committees raise different but equally difficult issues. The chair of the audit committee of a listed company in the post-Enron world is probably the most exposed Board non-exec. So many of the corporate scandals turn out to be accounting scandals. The chair of the audit committee is there to ensure that proper standards of accounting are maintained and that proper audits by independent auditors are carried out. The chair has to be numerate and has to have numerate people on the Board committee. The *UK Corporate Governance Code* requires there to be at least one non-executive on the audit committee "with recent and relevant experience".[2] But that does not have to be the chair. Indeed it may be better if the chair is more broadly business-oriented because the issues go wider than just accounting. An eminent Board chair told me that he treasured those accountants in his company who "focussed on the broader strategic picture and were not just number-crunchers".

Today some people are reluctant to take on audit committee membership because of the liabilities involved. But the risks are lessened by the fact that most of the time on the audit committee you are on the same side of the argument as the CFO, CEO and the executive.

A key role for the audit chair is to arbitrate between the auditors and the executives on points of disagreement in relation to the audited accounts. It can become quite heated trying to distinguish between capital and recurrent expenditure, between extraordinary and ordinary items and agreeing revenue/expenditure recognition policy – when is a sale a sale and when should the money from that sale and the expenditure related to that sale travel into the profit and loss account?

It is easy for audit committees to get lost in very technical detail, losing sight of the big ticket items such as debt levels and cash flow. Too high a level of debt can destroy a company when the unforeseen such as Covid suddenly happens. What constitutes too high a level of net debt is itself not an easy question to answer. Especially in boom years.

The fact that they are small committees compared with the larger Board itself should not lull the chairs of remco and audit into some idea that chairing is easier. Some of the most difficult committees and meetings to chair are the smallest. Good and experienced audit and remco chairs, good and experienced audit and remco members, are valuable commodities for any Board and demand careful recruiting.

Main Board meetings should always have on the agenda, close to the top, reports from committee chairs of meetings since the last Board – usually oral. In that way the sub-committees and the main Board are properly joined up. It also allows audit and remco chairs to get their key points across to the whole main Board, not just to the subset of their committee members.

NOMINATIONS COMMITTEE – NOMCO

The nominations committee (nomco) is normally a less contentious affair and meets much less often. It is concerned with selecting new Board members, both executive and non-executive. It is usually chaired by the main Board chair (unless the committee is seeking the chair's successor) and should be concerned with the succession plans for the Board. Many Boards do not spend enough time on succession planning. Nomco should encourage it and lead it – at risk of embarrassment with senior people, both executive and non-executive, who deem themselves irreplaceable.

One nominations sensitivity (beyond the sensitive task of replacing the chair) is the involvement of the executives in any selection of a new non-executive director. They should and must be involved, especially the CEO. But they have no veto.

Nomco is all about getting the people round the Board table right, as has been underlined in previous chapters. The next chapter on chairing selection panels is pure nomco territory.

ANNUAL GENERAL MEETINGS

Finally, a brief note on annual general meetings (AGMs). They are strange beasts. The annual chance for all and any shareholders (holding one share or more) to see the members of the Board in the flesh and to ask easy or awkward questions and vote for and against their plans, as appropriate. Sadly, the vast majority of AGMs are less than exciting because only a tiny number of small shareholders bother to turn up. There are usually more professional advisers and staff members in the room than actual shareholders. Big shareholders seldom turn up.

The key point for a chair who has not chaired an AGM before is having a good script, written almost certainly by the company secretary. The chair has to have a script which sets out what will be said by whom in terms of motions and the order of play. It is a scripted affair except for questions and answers. Stick to the script. And make time afterwards for tea with shareholders – they can give you a good, if serendipitous, temperature check.

REFERENCES

1. *UK Corporate Governance Code* (July 2018), London: Financial Reporting Council.
2. Ibid.

7

CHAIRING SELECTION PANELS

I really enjoy chairing or being on selection panels. You learn more about your fellow man or woman from selection panels than almost any other type of meeting. Not just about the candidates (the aim of the exercise) but also about those on the selection panel alongside you – people you may have worked with for some time already. A good head-hunter (recruitment consultant) adds enormous value but should not be allowed to be in charge.

A FALLIBLE BUSINESS

Selecting people is immensely fallible. One may get better at it with years of practice but even with practice we still make mistakes. A major reason is the format of the selection panel. Someone who is good at talking around a table may not be good at the actual job which involves much more than talking around a table. The selection methods of the War Office Selection Board (known as Wasbee) for becoming a National Service officer involved such things as how to get the team of real people you were put in charge of, across a river with a plank that was too short. Sitting round a table and talking favours the bull-shitter who can talk but not necessarily do. It favours the visionary rather than the finisher, the big picture person rather than someone with an attention to detail. The good CEO, as noted earlier, needs to be both proficient at 35,000 feet doing the vision thing and, simultaneously, able to handle the detail on the ground. Short planks crossing rivers potentially favour the doer not the talker.

LOGISTICS

Logistics are key to successful selection boards. If the interviews are held in the premises of a head-hunter, then the logistics are sorted out by them. The task is how to get the short-listed candidates not to meet and recognise each other in the course of the interview day. This becomes more and more important as the seniority of the job climbs. When I was interviewed for the job of chair of Ofcom, the selection board met in a government building. I quickly identified the other five candidates at the reception desk. The media had, as usual, not got the short-list right! I can read lists upside down.

With a selection board it is essential to have the right mix of people as the interviewers. If a new company Board member is being sought, I believe all Board members should feel fully involved in the appointment, even though not all Board members can do the final interviewing. The choice of interviewers will require diplomacy.

PUBLIC APPOINTMENTS

In UK public appointments such as choosing the next chair of the BBC or Ofcom, there is the good habit of having an independent external assessor who can bring a sensible outsider's view to the event. During my years as an independent external assessor of public appointments in London, I found that I was encouraged to bring the sort of distance that insiders may lose. Like a non-executive director on a company Board. The public appointments selection board has the task of choosing those candidates who are "appointable", allowing the minister or prime minister to make the final choice between the appointable candidates.

Sadly, in recent times the revered and independent public appointments system in the UK has become politicised. Ministers seek to intervene earlier in the process and choose on the basis of political loyalties rather than merit. Making public appointments that bypass any kind of selection process altogether is a clear breach of the established system – with chumocracy replacing democracy, as noted earlier.

A GOOD MIX OF INTERVIEWERS

The right mix of interviewers on an interview panel normally means a mix of soft and hard, supportive and challenging. The right mix also means taking diversity seriously. It is unfair on a woman candidate to be faced with a barrage of males. I remember my final interviews for my first job – at the BBC. The first interview was soft, with the interviewer agreeing with what I said in answers to his questions, smiling supportively. The second interview, which followed, absolutely threw me – he asked questions and gave no signal or sign or remote indication as to what might be the "right answer" and if he agreed with what I was saying. It took a while to regain equilibrium and realise that this was a hard interview(er).

PLANNING THE QUESTIONS

Make time before the first candidate arrives to go through the planned questions and make sure who on the selection panel is asking what question in what order. I make it a rule when chairing a selection panel that the same structure of questions broadly should face every candidate. It is easier and fairer to compare candidates if the same questions are asked. Interviewers should however be encouraged to fire supplementary questions unplanned at the candidate, following up the agreed questions which they or colleagues are asking. This breaks up what might become a rather rigid structure and tests the candidate more.

What questions to ask is very subjective. I like rather simple starters for ten such as: "Why did you apply for this post and what are your qualifications and skills for it?" I also like more off-the-wall questions: "What is the single achievement in your personal or professional life that you are most proud of?" One candidate a few years ago was an Olympic athlete. Asked that question, he twisted, rather embarrassed, crossed his knees and said: "It is not athletics". There was then a pause. And then a smile. "No, it is athletics …. When I looked up at my time, and saw that I had broken the World Record." He got the job and was a great Board member. Another example of less traditional backgrounds and experience coming up trumps.

I think it is also important to clear away the glasses and cups of tea used by the previous candidate. It is a bit like a hotel bedroom, you do not want to think that it has been used by someone else before. The candidate should be allowed to come in and start fresh.

"NAME-BLIND" SELECTION

In Northern Ireland, given concerns about sectarian favouritism in my experience, there were very strict rules in public appointments about the same questions being asked of all candidates (with little or no deviation for supplementaries); and about scoring the answers. When short-listing candidates based on their CVs and letters of application, the protocol required that candidates have numbers and not names, again to avoid sectarian bias. However, the whole point of anonymity was somewhat lost when my local Northern Irish assessor took one look at a particularly strong CV and said with a naughty smile – well of course, everyone knows her, No. 231 is Mary O'Leary.

With the aim of trying to reduce discrimination in recruitment – central to achieving greater diversity – more and more employers in the public and private sectors are selecting people for interview on a "name-blind" basis. This would seem to be fairer in that it reduces racial and sexual bias. I once had a CEO who as a boy growing up in working-class Glasgow, left school at 14 and could not get a job. A friend suggested changing his CV to a Protestant-sounding school, and he found employment the following day.

A university librarian in Australia told me that recruitment interviews across the university were not allowed to ask candidates about their age, ethnic origins or gender/sexuality. Yet from the top of the university came strong calls to encourage increased diversity when appointing academic and non-academic staff.

JUDGING THE CANDIDATES

Some selection board chairs do not like discussing the candidates until all have been seen – at the end. I have a different approach. I think it is a good idea to talk about the candidate while he or she is fresh in the mind. If it is the first candidate of the day, is he or she appointable? If not, discard. If it is the second or the third candidate, who is leading the pack? Who is at the moment – before any more candidates arrive – the preferred option, the one to beat?

The problem with selection boards is that they are so fallible, as noted at the outset. Being interviewed by four strange people in a strange room may not be any sort of proxy for the post and skills and competencies that are being sought. It may just tell you that she or he is good at being interviewed. Overly formal interviews can also discourage candidates from diverse backgrounds.

How can one overcome this fallibility or at least reduce it? There are three things that the chair can do.

References

First of all, read the references that are offered by the candidate (but of course they will be supportive). You and your colleagues may find it useful to identify some informal references – people who have known the candidate in the past. But check the approach with the HR team. The more people you know and trust, who know and trust the candidate and can give you views, the better. In my experience a consensus view of the person emerges which is consistent and truthful.

The night before the final interviews for a new CEO, I was at a party. By chance I found myself talking to a young woman who turned out to work for one of the favoured candidates. I asked her about him, without of course saying why. She laughed, shot to attention, pointed to the distance and said, "There – the sound of gunfire – we are marching towards it." He was selected on the following day and turned out to be a very good appointment.

"Fireside" chats

The chair of the selection panel can have one-to-one chats with all the candidates before the actual formal interview day. This deepens the experience. It also helps when, not unusually, the candidate needs to be wooed to come rather than the other way around. It also helps with younger, less experienced, less traditional candidates who can find selection panels daunting. When a very good CEO of mine was moving on to a bigger job, her number two told me he would not be applying for the job, being young and inexperienced. I persuaded him to apply if only because selection panels are always good practice. He was selected – and was a great successor.

Don't rush to judgement

Thirdly, do not rush to judgement on the interview day. If the decision needs more time, give it more time. I and my then chair were once faced with a very difficult decision between two very good people (one of whom was the head-hunter's preferred candidate). At the end of the formal interviews, one candidate was marginally ahead of the other but it was close. We invited the two people back on separate occasions to meet with us in a different setting. The decision after this was easy to make (and she turned out to be excellent). We went against the head-hunter's preference on this occasion.

PERSONAL ASSISTANTS

One final thought for the chair of selection boards. Informally ask the PAs and receptionists who have had to deal with the candidates before and after the formal interview, *their* views on the candidates. My (Ismaili Muslim) PA found a particular heavyweight candidate had treated her "in a patronising and discourteous manner". I had been treated royally. By their deeds, ye shall know them.

Good PAs are a boon to chairs of all types. They are good at below the radar navigation of important issues and of important people. The PA of my Government review of the Royal Mail hunted down some excellent office space for me and the review team. He had found it on the same floor, using the same lift, as the Secretary of State, ministers and the permanent secretary. This turned out to be a master stroke – not just because of access to the ministerial biscuit tin. Chance meetings in the lift were especially useful. The review from the beginning was treated as "ministerial level" since it was on the ministerial floor. People within the civil service and outside were delighted to be invited to review meetings and consultations. PAs getting details like office space right, either serendipitously or planned, can make large contributions to a chair's success.

8

CHAIRING CONFERENCES, SUMMITS AND DINNERS

CHAIRING CONFERENCES

Chairing a conference makes some special demands. But the need for preparation, and for audibility and visibility, is even stronger than when chairing an ordinary meeting. Double and triple check the conference audio-visual technology and make yourself known to the audio-visual team.

The key point about chairing a conference or a conference session is to remember that you are not there to expound *your* views. You are there to elicit good content from speakers and then good questions from the floor so that conference delegates feel that they are participating and not just on the receiving end of a chain of one-way transmissions. If you want to expound your views then get yourself invited to speak and not chair. Chairs should bring speakers and delegates together not drive them apart. Good chairs like good regulators should be suitably invisible and not attention-seeking.

At a big conference in Paris, the session chair was scheduled to make a few opening remarks (I would suggest to conference organisers that they avoid this as a general rule). The session chair's (not very interesting) remarks started as an acceptably small mountain spring suddenly became a waterfall and then a raging torrent. He was determined to make his mark before the (somewhat more illustrious) speakers began. Like many inexperienced speakers he had no sense of how much time he was taking. Before he knew where he was he had eaten up 20 minutes, 15 minutes more than scheduled. As the session began late, the net effect was that the first and keynote speaker began half an hour late and the last speaker (and audience) was most displeased to be squeezed.

There is a wonderful story about the Antarctic explorer Sir Ernest Shackleton, a renowned public speaker, addressing an audience in Carnegie Hall, New York. The date is 1917.

> The chairman, an elderly member of council, had never chaired a meeting before. What I presume had happened was that he had conferred with Shackleton, who had unfortunately given him all his points. The chairman stood up. Every time he mentioned Shackleton, who was alone, sitting back, the whole audience gave a rousing cheer. The chairman was encouraged and proceeded to give Shackleton's lecture. He spoke for 40 minutes before he could be pulled down. It was agony.[1]

At the start of a conference it is important to establish whether the Chatham House Rule (rule singular, not rules plural) will apply to all or any session.

> When a meeting, or part thereof, is held under the Chatham House Rule, participants are free to use the information received, but neither the identity nor the affiliation of the speaker(s), nor that of any other participant, may be revealed.

Stating the Chatham House Rule clearly and up-front, if relevant to the conference or session you are chairing, will reassure speakers that they can genuinely speak freely. The tricky part is defining the social media rules. People know that under Chatham House they cannot identify who said what in the press. But often people are mentioned on Twitter as "X saying Y during Z conference". More difficult to control in the digital world.

When it comes to the question and answer (Q & A) part of a session, the conference chair should learn to hold back. If the speaker finishes and the chair immediately comes in with a question (or worse, two questions one after the other), this has the effect of stopping or reducing questions from the floor. Delegates feel that they might as well leave it to the chair since he appears to know it all and they are not being asked. And delegates who are shy about asking a question in the first place become even more shy.

The conference session chair, instead of immediately jumping in with the first question, needs to actively encourage questions when the speaker has finished. The chair should leave a genuine and confident pause to allow questions to emerge from the floor. I sometimes will say something like: "We have a lot of experience not just up here on the platform but also amongst the delegates, so questions please or comments but please keep them short." Pause and scan the audience widely. If after a genuine pause, there are still no questions, it is of course incumbent on the chair to come in with an apt question. Better still, in the coffee break before a session that might be expected not to elicit immediate questions, prime a delegate or two whom you know and can trust and get them to ask that first icebreaking question. Once the ice is broken, I usually find questions can come quick and fast for the rest of the day, even from the less forward people in the room.

An experienced conference organiser has suggested:

> If you are short on time/are hosting a remote conference (much more likely these days) and have an experienced session chair, you could use the Sli.do app which enables audience members to submit questions during the session via their phones, direct to the session chair. The chair receives them on his iPad (or similar) and he can scroll through and choose the best ones. He can then either ask the audience member to ask it, or to save time, ask it for them. This is another way of avoiding bad/long questions from audience members who just want their voice heard and waste valuable session time.

Some conference chairs are very rigid about not allowing comments or mini speeches from the floor, only bona fide questions. But my view is that in most conferences it is a risk worth taking; plus it also stops people dressing up a comment as a question in an artificial and slightly tedious way.

But what do you do about the conference bore (the reason why most chairs do not allow mini speeches from the floor)? He or she *will* want to make a speech from the floor which usually adds little value, goes on too long and/or is off the point. The chair will have to stop the speech forcefully; and a good audio-visual team will kill the mike at the same time. As for handling the bore's second, third and fourth questions, ignore the hand or search vigorously in the semi darkness for another hand, any hand will do. Fortunately, the chance of there being two bores in the same hall is, in my experience, as likely as lightning striking the conference centre twice.

Sometimes of course, there are some really smart people in the audience who are relevant to the session. Good preparation knowing who the delegates are, or prompts from the conference organisers, can enable the chair to hand-pick a couple of top delegates and ask them their views. This can add energy/controversy to the on-stage panel conversation. Boring one-way transmission is thus avoided.

One other reminder about questions. In conferences, seminars and big meetings, it never does any harm to ask people in the audience with questions, to say who are they are and where they are from, before they ask a question or give a comment. I sometimes make a gentle joke: "Please say who you are and where you come from physically, politically or philosophically ...."

Asking questioners to introduce themselves from the floor is courteous to the speakers and assists with the networking that lies at the heart of good conferences. Some chairs imagine in some rather elitist way that everyone who is anyone knows everyone who is anyone and therefore introductions are not needed. Do not follow this. Just because the few celebrity people in the meeting know each other and are probably known to others in the audience does not mean that the chair should not ask people to identify themselves before they speak – including the celebrities. Incidentally, you have to be careful if you as chair point and name a delegate because you know her. Noses will then be out of joint if, when you call their owners, you have forgotten their names or never knew them. I tend to point to the well-known person with hand raised and ask them to introduce themselves. It is safer in the longer run. *Good chairing is mostly about the longer run.*

Quite a few conference chairs have the habit of going to the audience and taking three questions at once from three different people – especially towards the end of a conference session when time's wing-èd chariot is flying through the air. The speaker and/or the panel usually forget one or other of the questions, and the questioner rightly feels hard done by. I would prefer the chair, even towards the end of a busy session, to stick to one question at a time but take them quickly.

One point about mikes in Q&A sessions. It is essential to have roving mikes and it is essential to make sure that those holding the mikes and moving them around the hall watch you on the podium so that they know which is the next hand to go to. Roving wireless mikes are also technology cock-ups waiting to happen. Make sure they are working and switched on when handed to questioners and ensure that there are back-ups. In a big room one working roving mike is just useless and very time-consuming. Do not necessarily encourage the mike holders to snatch away the mike from the questioner after the question is asked. It is often quite productive to ask the questioner whether he or she is satisfied with the answer from the speaker/panel. This is useless if the mike has already travelled 50 metres to the next hand held up. The occasional supplementary question from the questioner in the audience puts a bit of useful needle into sessions and keeps speakers on the podium on their toes, especially speakers who make a career out of not answering the question. One digital organisation had its audience mike set in a square rubber ball which could be thrown literally from audience member to audience member, thus speeding up matters, and adding some perhaps needed jollity.

But I have slightly run ahead of myself in dealing with Q&A sessions. There are other important points to watch with the speakers, before you get to the questions.

Timing

Make sure you have met the speakers before the session begins and make sure you tell them how long they are expected to speak, where they are expected to sit before their speech (usually in the hall itself at the front) and where on the platform they should sit after their speech. It is important to have good relationships with the conference organisers because it is their job to find the speakers and bring them to you.

Conference organisers, helpfully, often put session chairs in contact with their panellists well ahead of time. Chairs can then run through how the session will work via emails or phone calls and agree who is going to say what, in what order and what the key themes of the session are.

The bane of conference chairs (and conference organisers) is speakers who overrun. To compound the nuisance, the overrunners can be the less good speakers. Some speakers have absolutely no time sense at all. I remember a speaker who went on for 20 minutes. When I talked with him afterwards he genuinely thought he had spoken for half the time.

Conference organisers can be asked to provide a countdown clock on stage that kicks off when the session starts – session chairs and speakers/panellists therefore know exactly how long they have and cannot feign ignorance. One conference organiser said: "We genuinely kick people off stage if they run over their time."

But with most speakers, it pays to be courteously fierce. I have used to good effect a colleague in the audience sitting right in front of, and facing, the speaker. Two pieces of paper are held up discreetly - "Two Minutes To Go" and "Finish Now, Thanks". This is more human and, because clocks have a way of being ignored, can be more effective.

My first job as a BBC radio producer taught me a strong sense of time. You learn quickly what 1 minute 40 seconds is and you never lose that awareness. According to BBC guidelines, a typical speaker should do about 180 words a minute, three words a second. A typical A4 page is three to four minutes. This is a useful guide if you get to see the speaker's prepared text and become alarmed not just at the number of slides but also at the number of pages. I myself find 180 words sometimes a bit rushed and usually plan for fewer words a minute. People speaking too quickly can cause audibility problems as words elide – especially in echoey spaces.

A staff member who worked in the White House with President Ronald Reagan told me of a day when the President was dozing in the Oval Office. Walking into the Oval Office, he stirred the President and showed him a media briefing which needed to be delivered 20 minutes later – speaking for 1 minute 40 seconds. Twenty minutes later – 1 minute 40 seconds exactly. Reagan knew his comms.

Allegedly, President Reagan's favourite joke was: "As Jesus Christ said at the Last Supper, if you want to get in the picture come round my side of the table". I relayed this to a vicar I met who, rather than be affronted, promptly put it in her next sermon.

It is worth reminding speakers diplomatically that adding jokes or off-the-cuff remarks to a prepared speech, *lengthens it*. Speakers sometimes assume that the added bits on the day do not take extra time. They do. Always more than you think. But good jokes and good off-the-cuff remarks can also keep speeches energetic and fresh so chairs should not be too strict.

Have clear rules about stopping the speakers before they overrun. The one exception to this is the speaker who is clearly delighting the audience. Such speakers tend to be very good at timing so it does not happen very often. There are also occasional grands fromages who cannot be stopped however long they go on for.

The Emmy and Oscar award ceremonies (television and movie awards) in Los Angeles have a very effective way of stopping the award winners' thank-you speeches from overrunning the clearly allotted time – the bane of awards dinners. The producers just bring the music up ever more loudly, drowning out the words. Some of the stars are immensely irritated to be drowned out by music. Especially when, as on one occasion in 2004, at the Emmys, one star and one star alone did not get the music treatment – the star of Mike Nicholls' award-winning television blockbuster *Angels in America* – Al Pacino. Mr Pacino was allowed to talk and talk. Angel in America. Exceptional speaker. Grand fromage.

Do ask the speakers when you meet them first how long they intend to speak for. Even in well-run conferences, there can be mistakes. The speaker may have been told a different length by the conference organisers to what you have been told. Do also, if you can, peep at the speakers' PowerPoints (as well as the length of their prepared text). One speaker said he was going to speak (without a written text) for ten minutes and had 50 PowerPoint slides. I told him that this was not humanly possible and he kindly cut them down and stuck to his ten minutes. All PowerPoint corrupts, absolute PowerPoint corrupts absolutely.

When introducing a speaker, if the speaker's CV is in the conference delegates' pack, don't waste valuable conference time reading it out. This is a bad habit which is quite unnecessary and can in my experience go on for three or four dreary minutes. A short sharp intro injects momentum into the proceedings. But it is amazingly difficult to get speakers to go to the rostrum as soon as you start introducing them. Even when I have told them that this is what is required, and that my intros are very short indeed, speakers will still tend to sit tight until the introduction is over, pause and then go to the rostrum. This loses time and momentum. And if you are not careful, the speaker then tries to find the right buttons for their PowerPoint presentation, wasting more valuable time or they decide they need a neck mike.

Neck mikes are great for good speakers, allowing them to rove the stage. For less experienced speakers, it may be better to keep them chained to the rostrum's fixed mike. But remind them not to look right or left whilst speaking with a fixed mike as they will go off mike.

I once had to deal with a rather vain and egotistical speaker who demanded that I read out some four pages of handwritten introduction extolling the various virtues of said speaker. I refused and did my short intro. A quick decision, not exactly popular with the speaker, but right for the audience.

Finally, conference chairs today have to deal with speakers who are also sponsors of the conference. Twenty years ago conferences made their money purely from delegate fees. Now these are significantly supplemented by sponsorship and exhibition revenues, spex in the jargon. In exchange for money, the sponsor gets the logo on the wall, in the programme, in the conference brochure and also probably gets a speaking (or chairing) slot. The problem facing the conference organiser, and therefore the chair, is to prevent the sponsor speaker from just doing a sales pitch. Nothing is more likely to annoy conference delegates, especially if they have paid a thousand pounds to attend.

Once upon a time at a conference in Madrid, the sponsor speaker, a senior Vice President of a well-known technology firm, was asked to speak for 20 minutes at the beginning of the day – a keynote. He began late by 10 minutes (a sloppy chair and not his fault) and after about 20 very rambling minutes suddenly complained, to everyone's amazement and bemusement, that he had got the wrong slides and blamed the conference organiser. He then, instead of stopping, proceeded to speak for another rambling 20 minutes, oblivious to the annoyance in the hall made up of senior people and serious buyers. The esteem due to his brand and company was in disarray by the time the main session got started some three quarters of an hour late.

SUMMITS

The Church of England asked me on two occasions to chair and facilitate a residential seminar-cum-summit at St George's, Windsor Castle – senior members of the Church led by the Archbishop of Canterbury, meeting with senior members of the media led by the Director General of the BBC. The topic: how to handle the media.

The chair's task at a summit is to facilitate the exchange of views and opinions held by others – not his or her own. Ego has to be suppressed more deeply than with conference chairing.

The key here is elucidating and re-emphasizing what the (exam) question is, and steering participants away from too much serendipitous stray. Also key is clarifying one "side's" view to the other but not taking sides, in particular when the sides do not appear to be understanding each other. Logical discontinuities can be probed in the arguments put forward on every side by an independent-minded facilitator. This can be quite robust on occasion. Facilitation does *not* mean Softness. Facilitation does *not* mean Anything Goes.

Whilst it is important for chairs to try and ensure the right people are at a meeting, it is absolutely crucial for facilitators. If the right people are found and invited and accept, then the task of facilitation is made so much easier. The problem with some facilitations is that the top people whom you need will only come if they are given a speaking slot – this has to be handled diplomatically when there are more top people in the room than speaking slots in the programme. Speaking slots in facilitated seminars (as distinct from chaired conferences) can be a real disadvantage, as they can become unwieldy and attention-seeking. A speaking slot in a facilitated seminar is there to, with great brevity, create debate and open the topic – not close it off with ex cathedra statements.

One of the distinct advantages of getting the right mix of people to come to the summit meeting is that the chair/facilitator can lean back and allow the debate to flow from one side to the other, and to the third side, with relatively few interventions required.

A good facilitator should make sure that the conversation is not hogged by a small group of people (for example those who "won" speaking slots) and must open it up to the less forthcoming in the room. It is my experience as a chair, that some of the most productive interventions come from the quietest participants if they are allowed in and are encouraged to speak – a running theme of the book. They usually do not speak for long thus winning the prize for brevity. Probably because they have actually been listening to the others rather than focusing on their own next speechette, the quieter people can be quite decisive. I remember a Content Board meeting at Ofcom, when we were adjudicating a serious breach of the broadcasting code of practice. Before making our adjudication, I asked a member known for her quietness, her conclusion. "Child abuse on national radio." Five words. Decisive.

Seating plans

Facilitators of summits should get involved in the seating plan, just as they get involved in the invitations to participants. The key point is to get the participants, if at all possible, to see each other face to face, rather than sit face to back. The best seating plan is the half moon/ half circle where there can be maximum face to face eye to eye contact. The fewer rows the better to reduce the face to back problem. This layout is also good for audibility. Try and ensure that if there are "sides", that they do not sit together and that they sit interspersed. This facilitates real communication both during the session and then during the coffee breaks and meals.

The seating plan should try and avoid mimicking the differing views. The adversarial Punch and Judy nature of British politics is encouraged by the seating plan of the House of Commons.

I experienced one rather unusual outcome of a half-moon/half-circle single row seating arrangement when I was chairing a debate on the media with an advanced clergy course, also as it happens at St George's, Windsor Castle. I took as a case study a recent regulatory decision that had just been published and asked this representative group of mid-career clergy their view. I explained the background and then asked each person one by one their view, starting on my left, their right. The first three or four on my left, their right, took a very hard line conservative view of the decision (the regulator had got it wrong), the middle three or four were rather undecided, and to my amazement the last three or four on my right, their left, took a very liberal/libertarian view (the regulator had got it right). Had the seating positions from right to left over the course of two hours somehow hardened/softened their views?

At the Church of England/media summits at Windsor Castle it was important to get the bishops and the media people to intermingle in the half-moon/half-circle seating plan from the start and not sit in phalanxes. The discussions took place in the wonderful but not always good-for-audibility Vicars' Hall, built in 1415 – the fleur de lys in the carpet commemorating Henry V's victory over the French at the Battle of Agincourt. As a chair facing yet another meeting, it does sometimes feel like "Once more into the breach, dear friends, once more …".

COMMUNICATION AND MUNICATION

The danger of so many discussions and debates, whatever the context, is that people will be working on their own speech or their own next question, and not truly listening to the current speaker and current conversation. I remember with dread a European Union (EU) conference in Manchester where people from all over Europe talked past each other for two whole days, intent on making the speeches from the floor that they had prepared before they came, whether or not they related to the topics under scrutiny at the time. There was no communication, just a lot of munication. I, a novice in such matters, asked my EU-literate colleague whether this was normal. She said it was. The speeches would be recorded verbatim in the journal of record thus proving back in the home country the speakers' status and wisdom (and authorising their expenses-paid attendance).

DON'T EAT INTO LUNCH

Chairs should also remember that the breaks between sessions can sometimes be as or more valuable than the actual sessions themselves.

That is why chairs who let sessions overrun and eat into lunch or coffee break are so unpopular. As well as coming for the talks, people also come to conferences and summits to meet and network with other people. Video and audio conferencing do not offer this. How this will work in the future with more virtual chairing and more home working (Chapter 9) is not at all clear.

I find it quite useful in a facilitation to probe each side by asking them what would be their view of the theme/topic if they were, for the sake of argument, on the other side. There is an element of role-playing that can be encouraged by the facilitator – the bishops understanding what goes through the mind of the broadcaster on breaking news, for example. The broadcasters understanding that the Church of England does not have one standard policy view on every topic. Church of England people hold a wide range of views, well beyond the comfort zone of the typical current affairs programme with its dualistic time-driven demands for impartiality – yes no, for and against.

SUMMARISING

One other skill is useful to a chair/facilitator – the art of summarising the day's or afternoon's play. It does require hard work and it does mean that you have little if any time to lean back. I keep notes of key points made and by whom, and of some of the lighter moments, and then, if it is appropriate, play back rapid fire the words to everyone, quoting people by name, before the session ends. This is especially useful if there has been growth of an agreement during the facilitation, real progress in understanding that can be mapped. It can be very powerful in tying up loose ends and leaving key thoughts in people's minds and key questions yet to be addressed. It can also be fun. If the session is to continue after the break or in the morning, the summary can act as the starting point for the next stage.

CHAIRING DINNERS

I have had the pleasure of chairing a dining club in past years, The Pluralists. Pluralists are people who have a portfolio career, that is to say combining membership of a couple of company Boards with consultancy to a range of different clients. Not one employer but many – concurrently.

I chose a 7 7 4 4 seating plan round the club table as distinct from 8 8 2 2. Avoiding long and thin. This became popular with other dinners hosted in the same location.

Chairing dinners involving some kind of plenary public discussion not just nuclear conversations has some special challenges. The main one is kitchen, serving and other extraneous noise. If you are going to have a plenary discussion or speeches mid-meal, then ambient noise is incredibly annoying and can significantly reduce enjoyment and contribution. My audibility obsession again. Ideally a private room will solve most of this problem but it still needs managing with the staff serving the meal. Make sure that the kitchen is not next door, as happened in one central London location – my pre-dinner visit to the site had coincided with a morning when the kitchen was not active.

Never underestimate the power of sod's law. I was a keynote speaker at an Amsterdam banquet 30 years ago which involved a complicated entrance routine from the back of the hall. We practised it carefully. It all worked brilliantly until I got to the stage and opened my mouth – mike not working, thus destroying the whole slightly over-elaborate production plan. In between the time of the rehearsal and the performance (about 15 minutes), someone had by the sheerest of chances stood on a cable and the mike had come out of its plug.

At The Pluralists the plenary discussion took place over the main course with the door closed and waiters allowed in sparingly to refill glasses – thus audibility and focus are maximised. Most dinners hold any speech and/or plenary session over coffee which is advantageous as regards noise (assuming waiters have been asked to clear away the plates quietly). But this can reduce the time spent on discussion. Also the coffee course is a long time to wait for the meat of the meeting and makes the whole event much longer. Most dinner guests want to be away by 10pm in these busy days, from a start around 7.30pm.

After-dinner speakers

This is not a book about after-dinner speaking which would require its own separate volume. But as chair of a dinner you need to think hard about managing the after-dinner speaker, especially if she or he is not particularly good at it. After-dinner is the most difficult form of public speaking. Length is again – as in conference chairing – the key. A poor but short after-dinner speech will usually be quickly forgiven, but not a poor long one. At a dinner in Cambridge the chair must have felt pretty relaxed about the after-dinner speaker (he told me afterwards he was). The speaker was a well-known television celebrity. The problem was that after 10 minutes the celebrity was not being funny, and made the unwise decision to go on digging for another 15 minutes of embarrassment. If you are chairing an after-dinner speaker, do firmly establish the length of the speech and encourage even the good speakers to stick to it. It is said that on your death-bed you are unlikely to look back on your life and regret that after-dinner speakers did not spend more time speaking.

You may find it a good idea to put your less experienced after-dinner speaker before the dinner or after, say, the first course. This is especially useful if the speaker is not a great joke-smith.

With non-professional after-dinner speakers, it may be a good idea to discuss with them beforehand whether they intend to make jokes. There are some speakers who are just not good at jokes but feel somehow duty-bound in an after-dinner speech to make some. I encourage these people to leave out the jokes and stick to the knitting. A short and serious after- (or before-) dinner speech is held in much higher regard than a longer speech with failed jokes. My difficulty with some after-dinner comedy speakers is that they tell joke after joke after joke in a breath-taking way but there may be no real content at all that is relevant to that audience. Most dinner audiences like some content with their coffee.

Seating plans

A good seating plan materially contributes to the success of a dinner which you are chairing. It requires thought and can of course be fraught with possible mistakes. Some nationalities tend to put husbands and wives, partners and spouses side by side whereas the English always separate them.

The problem with seating plans is people can feel stuck after a couple of courses, having said everything worth saying. Chairing a dinner, I often move people at some point. This needs planning to avoid putting the wrong people together after the move. Done well, it supercharges the occasion. At a recent dinner, the dessert was served from a buffet so people could choose their own seating plan. Or chat standing.

Finally a cautionary tale. Many businesses now use private dinners for corporate marketing purposes – in exotic places and private restaurants. On one occasion, a business had hired something of a celebrity to chair the dinner on the reasonable assumption that he would be a pied piper attracting good attendees. He came late, probably drank too much, complained that he would have preferred being elsewhere that night and then complained about the quality of the food and wine. I think if you are seriously chairing, no or just a little alcohol steadies the hand on the tiller. You never know when there might be a storm.

A BRAVE NEW WORLD

Let us now take this story of chairing meetings to the final chapter of the book. A new and unexpected world as a result of the Covid pandemic. Chairing virtual meetings not physical meetings.

REFERENCE

1.   Fisher, M. and Fisher, J. (1957), *Shackleton*, London: Barrie Books.

9

VIRTUAL CHAIRING – THE FUTURE? THE NEXT NORMAL?

"Doorbells ringing, children wandering and dogs barking …."
"You need a chair – way more than normal."

The first draft of this book was being completed in February 2020 BC (Before Covid). An additional final chapter emerged, as working from home and lockdowns became the norm across the world.

Audio and video conferencing, old-style, are basically physical meetings with technology added. They have been around a long time.

But the new world of technology platforms, such as Zoom and Microsoft Teams, creates virtual not physical meetings and the need for virtual not physical chairing. These platforms work at the megabit and gigabit speeds of today's broadband optic fibre networks. Digital technology is not just added to a meeting as in audio and video conferencing, but becomes central and critical to the operation of the meeting – becomes the platform on which the meeting works.

These are early days for the new technologies but lessons are emerging. Becalmed by chance in a rural part of South Australia as Covid ramped up elsewhere, I asked (consulted!) a number of my international friends and colleagues to share their experiences of virtual chairing and being virtually chaired. This final chapter summarises the main points a virtual chair needs to understand – from their and my experience. The voices quoted are those of CEOs, chairs, managers and consultants, across a range of organisations, from companies to trade associations, professional associations and public sector bodies, in the UK and beyond. It was a telecoms executive in New Zealand who suggested that, in her view, the "new normal" is more likely to be the "next normal"! She also introduced me to the phrase IRL – in real life.

This last chapter – dealing with an uncertain present and future for chairs of meetings – required a different style to the rest of the book: a mosaic of voices and views.

TECHNOLOGY PLATFORMS

A growing range of platforms exist for virtual chairing and virtual meetings. Zoom and Microsoft Teams are the platforms that appear to be most popular. There are many more, for example Webex, Google Handouts, Google Meets, Bluejeans, Houseparty, Miro. Some platforms, like Bluejeans, are felt to be useful for more social events.

> I regularly use Zoom, Microsoft Teams, and Google Meets across PC, tablet and mobile. My favourite is Zoom on PC. You are notified when people are waiting to be admitted to the meeting, it is extremely easy to schedule, and excellent quality and reliability …. Zoom seems to be the 'Switzerland' of video technology … it doesn't irritate anyone and seems to have ubiquitous reach and appeal to old, young, tech savvy, luddite.
>
> Google Meets is my second favourite. Again, high adoption but not universal (UK civil servants apparently aren't allowed to use it) and simple to use. Good quality screen-sharing works very well.
>
> Microsoft Teams seems to be the public sector technology of choice – I'm told because it has proven higher security credentials. However I find it clunky which doesn't make for straightforward conversations. Perhaps I've just been unlucky, but a quick straw-poll tends to agree it's the least user-friendly of the mainstream video technology platforms.

FAMILIARISE YOURSELF

The first and most obvious thing the virtual chair has to do, faced with the range of meeting platforms, is to:

Familiarise yourself. Just as you would with a meeting room or event space; make sure that you know your way around the platform you are using. Does it have a hand-raise function, where is the chat, who has the power to mute participants, what does the presenter view look like, how does it look and feel to the audience? The differences from Zoom to Microsoft Teams to Webex may be subtle but they are critical.

There is a limit to how many active people one can have in a Microsoft Teams meeting.

TECHNOLOGY TIME-WASTERS

Chairs in the world of physical meetings need to get the technology right, for example microphones and slide presentations, as discussed in Chapter 1. In the virtual world getting the technology right is critical – "must have" not "nice to have". Technology problems in a physical meeting are a nuisance. They destroy a virtual meeting:

> There are instances of unreliable connectivity, buffering and freezing of screens at best and a digital wipe-out at worst. Yes, the broadband networks have undeniably held up remarkably well but we have all been in meetings where some erratic connectivity issues have disrupted the flow of the discussion.

NEW LEARNING NEEDED

Chairs must bear in mind that the new virtual technology can quickly exclude those who are not technologically literate or able, not confident. Physical meetings in physical spaces are by contrast straightforward and naturally inclusive. Time needs to be devoted outside, before and during meetings to help all members of the meeting to understand the tools available on the various platforms, to avoid exclusion. At a recent Zoom meeting I had forgotten where the video on/off button was (which removes or adds your picture). A colleague quickly intervened and told me where to find it on the Zoom screen.

Covid has forced us into learning new tools/platforms. Use the tools/platforms you already have available (but haven't bothered to learn) and use the new tools/platforms coming available!

Many people think that the use of the new video platforms is just an extension of video conferencing between meeting rooms at different locations. Once these people have nailed how to dial in, mute and unmute their voices, they are done. But it is not the same. These are different platforms and you have to learn to switch between them!

Different platforms can help you do different things such as, for example, 'raise hand – I want to speak'. You have to take the time to learn and try to then make all this part of the 'normal'. The hand-raise function on the Zoom platform is hidden less than intuitively under Participants, at the bottom of the screen. Once clicked it appears top right of the screen.

The people who are fully utilising the tool offered by the various platforms are the ones who tend to have agile mind-sets. They are comfortable with uncertainty and the tools and frameworks have the structure to lead them to where they need to be and to focus on a human-centred approach. If you don't know how to get the presentation up on Zoom, organise beforehand for someone who does know how to do it and be there – or be taught and get confident. 'Practice makes permanent.'

'Practice makes permanent' is excellent advice to all types of chairs in all types of meetings. "The harder I practise, the luckier I get", as quoted at the beginning of this book in the Introduction.

MEETING PREPARATION

Chairing on Microsoft Teams means winging it isn't an option.

A running theme in this book is for the chairs and those in the chair's team/the secretariat to spend time on preparation. At this early stage in the life cycle of the new virtual technology, virtual meetings certainly need preparation even more than physical meetings:

Few chairs print the agenda, hand out badges and drive the slide-deck in physical meetings; the same is true in the virtual world. Make sure you have a good understanding with the secretariat what is expected of them and how they are preparing for it. How has the invite been set up? Will attendees join muted automatically or not? Will they enter a lobby and who will admit them? Will they make a noise when they join? All things that can and should be tailored to individual meetings.

Do a trial run with a new platform. For our first Board meeting back in March, my chair and I did a practice Zoom meeting for 20 minutes the day beforehand, just to ensure he was comfortable with the various layout options, how to mute/unmute (top tip: press the space bar as an un-mute shortcut!), and his own appearance … he's not vain, just wanted to see what others would see! Before every Board meeting, my chair and I always connect on Zoom ten minutes beforehand – just as we would always both be physically in the boardroom before others arrived. Small talk is definitely harder on screen, but light commentary about current affairs and the good old weather still seem to work while everyone gathers.

MEETING ETIQUETTE

The chair needs to set out clearly the etiquette for the meeting, the house-keeping rules to be followed.

Do you want attendees to put their hands up, or say that they would like to intervene via the chat function (recommended?) Would you like attendees to turn off their video and go on mute when they are not speaking? This I recommend. Non-video users tend to be shuffled out of view so that it is clearer who is talking. Do you want to ask people to turn on their video when speaking?

More guidance on the boundaries of the meeting needs to be given up-front: Is it or is it not ok to turn the video off? Is it expected that the mute button is off when you are not speaking? If you are eating lunch at the same time, please go on mute as you will make the rest of us hungry! Stick to x minutes please and state what page number you are on – presenters, you need to get more structured too. People actually like clarity so this is an opportunity to be very clear on expectations – at every meeting. Encourage people to dial in early in case they have a technical challenge – then there is more chance of starting on time – and less chance of people being late on to the call. Alternatively, decide if you will allow five minutes or so at the start because you expect someone will have trouble getting in, switching from what they were on before the call. If you can explain to a five year old how things should go, then you have it about right – clear, simple, easy to follow.

More patience is needed: 'You're on mute' rings out on a regular basis. In addition to work and home blending into one, people are also switching devices and headsets using different online tools/platforms for different meetings. This is 'new time' that gets eaten up in their day AND 'brain time' that gets eaten up which they didn't have to expend before.

More focus is needed by everyone on the call: so meetings must have more breaks and be shorter overall. We have to work much harder to 'feel' what is going on for others. And if it's a call where you can't see everyone in a grid on the screen, you have to scroll across to get a check every now and again of facial expressions etc.

INCLUSIVE MEETINGS

A real advantage of virtual meetings, compared with physical meetings, is that "the loudest cannot simply intervene and hog the conversation". Perhaps surprisingly.

There must be more awareness to be inclusive and bring everyone into the conversation actively and efficiently at the right points. Round table check-ins or pulling in the person who has said nothing.

There needs to be more opportunity for everyone to be on an even footing: meetings are better if everyone is 'all in the room', 'all on the video' or 'all on the phone'. When you have a mixture of virtual and physical meetings at play, the people who are virtual may have less influence/impact, for example than those sitting together in a room.

This last point was raised in Chapter 1 in relation to traditional audio conferencing. Chairs forget the invisible members phoning in and favour those that she or he can see around the table.

THE CHAT FUNCTION

The chat function can be an extremely powerful accompaniment for the chair; make sure you keep an eye on it!

In physical meetings "one and one only conversation" has been emphasised, with the chair sitting on side-mutterings. The chat function available in virtual meeting needs some rules:

Set the boundaries. The chat shouldn't take away from the main debate. Set out the boundaries of what you want at the start. Side conversations should be taken elsewhere.

Use the chat to stack questions until the end of presentations – to allow for greater flow of conversation.

Use the chat to engage shy or reticent participants who may otherwise not have engaged.

Minute the chats – they are part of the meeting and treat them as such.

TIPS/ADVICE

I always use two laptops for virtual meetings, one for the papers and one for the actual meeting. I have to be better organised and this helps me run things better.

Pause. Get used to pauses. Ask a panellist or member to come in but all you hear is silence? They may well be struggling to find the mute/unmute button – so pause for slightly longer than is natural in a physical meeting before moving on.

Keep it short. Generally, aim to run your virtual meeting two thirds shorter than your physical meeting. Staring at a screen is tiring, be concise and save us all from tired eyes and ears.

People need a lesson in camera angles!

The most effective chairs are constantly scanning the faces and expressions of all attendees, and the smartest attendees use body language to signal they wish to intervene. One of my best non-exec directors will physically raise her hand for a few seconds to ensure the chair knows she wishes to comment at the next opportunity … the crucial requirement is that the chair can see everyone's face on screen (top tip: the bigger your screen, the more faces will be visible, so as chair, get a big screen!).

From what I have seen this year, the most effective chairs of virtual meetings adopt a more scripted approach to their comments – their introduction is precise and thoughtful, the house-keeping is clear, apologies from those absent, minutes, etc are done efficiently, and there is a clear purpose and narrative about the meeting up front. No doubt that's all best practice IRL (in real life), but perhaps it's actually even easier to 'script' opening and closing remarks when you're chairing virtually because no one can see that you're reading?

On a practical note – we schedule a five-minute comfort break in the middle of our three-hour Board meetings. Five minutes is usually more like eight minutes by the time everyone is back, but I think telling people they have ten minutes would mean they would take twelve minutes and that is too long.

Over the past few months I have experimented with what I wear on video calls. This might sound daft, but my conclusion is that if I wear a suit jacket, I have a more effective meeting – I believe this gives a more business-like impression to the other attendees and shows that I am serious. I have never really dressed scruffily, but on my more relaxed days I find my virtual meetings have a more informal tone. So that old adage – dress for the job you want, not the job you've got – is perhaps still true in a digital world. I quietly judge others who are wearing sports clothes or clearly haven't brushed their hair! My chair admitted that he even sprays aftershave before his virtual meetings!

Above all, having a secretariat to help co-ordinate and deliver the sessions is essential. This is to ensure that you are chairing effectively. Being able to focus on the discussion in hand – particularly when this becomes less audible with background activity or faulty earphones – and not having to simultaneously take notes, is particularly invaluable. As are the additional eyes and ears to signal that there are hands raised or comments and questions in the chat function that need attention. It also helps to vary the tone and pitch of the meeting if your agenda is organised so that you have presenters both from your own team and from your target audience.

I believe 'Zoom fatigue' is a real thing! Back to back meetings, when you're glued to a screen all day every day, can fatigue even the most energetic person. So I now only schedule my most important client meetings on an otherwise quiet day so that I can give 100% and don't come across as weary!

KEEPING ATTENTION

Even the most diligent attendee will be tempted to glance at an email or the news. Recap key points for those who may have switched off. Use slides or visual aids to force attendees back to the conference call once in a while.

DEALING WITH INTERRUPTIONS

Doorbells ringing, children wandering and dogs barking ....

Video conferencing is fantastic in many ways, but particularly with Covid, it offers you a portal into someone's home life rather than their office life. Interruptions therefore will occur. If it is disruptive, make sure you or colleagues can mute attendees … but otherwise embrace it.

WHAT ARE THE GOOD AND NOT SO GOOD THINGS ABOUT THE NEW VIRTUAL CHAIRING PLATFORMS?

It is good for connections and transactions, good for management updates, good for teams and customers – way better than a telephone call. It's tough for new customer meetings, tough for hard negotiations, tough for new joiners to feel the culture, impossible for senior recruitment.

The good

At the outset I suspected that the chairing of meetings could become somewhat hollow and depersonalised without the pleasantries in coffee areas, casual chats in lifts or foyers. But in general these concerns seem to have been largely unfounded. By arriving early to the meetings there is often opportunity for some of the familiar greetings and personal engagement. And for those who choose to use the camera function in meetings, particularly when you are chairing less than 25 in a session, this presents a human counterpoint to what could be a more sterile environment.

We do all our meetings on Microsoft Teams – including hearings with the parties (maybe 50 or 60 people on the call). From a technical perspective, it's all fine. Everybody has got the hang of dealing with signals dropping, feedback etc., and we all quickly learnt how to use the mute buttons and so on. So, we get through the agenda, as normal, we arrive at decisions and the processes seem on the whole pretty normal.

On the plus side I've found there is greater adherence to timings on an agenda – there is a greater discipline with interventions from those around the virtual table. And whilst there is largely the same back and forth of discussion, there often appears to be less labouring of points. Interestingly I also found that a few participants who didn't actively engage in physical sessions have found it easier to engage in virtual meetings. There are no eyes on you around the virtual table, and there appears to be a greater sense of self-awareness leading to less grand-standing by others. In a sense one could argue that an online presence can be a great leveller. Of course you can of course play God and mute everyone on the call, which is often a pre-requisite for larger meetings or conferences. That is an instant, albeit temporary leveller!

I have also found that forging human connections can be much more authentic and intimate in a virtual world, as surprising as that sounds. For example, I recently participated in a small meeting with six Members of Parliament all interested in my company – now I know the name of their pet cat, 'met' one of their children, and told them about my love of sailing because they could see some sailing books over my shoulder on a bookcase! That sort of personal connection would not have been possible if I was darting in and out of their parliamentary offices on the Thames Embankment and battling their special political advisers!

There is a better attendance rate, especially for the local government audit committee that I chair (where quoracy is an issue).

A meeting is quorate when there are sufficient members present to discuss and make decisions/cast votes – as laid down in the rules of that organisation.

The not so good

The thing you miss most is the camaraderie – the other people. (And the cakes and biscuits.)

In a physical meeting, non-verbal communication between members can play an important, often less recognised, role. Raised eyebrows, glances, shrugs, the unspoken spoken – can elicit agreement/disagreement from the other side of the table and redirect the course of the meeting and its decisions. There is an understated mutuality, not necessarily involving the chair, which is missing in screen meetings. This is especially true where people have worked together a long time and know each other well.

It's not good for strategic or discursive discussion. As chair you want to be able to see who is itching to get in on a particular point, to keep the flow of the conversation on the same track, to keep its energy. The necessary formality makes it suitable for functional decision-making, less good for looser conversations. It's OK for Boards who can automatically draw on knowledge of each other garnered from months'/years' worth of meetings where you chat over the coffee urn, sandwich lunch etc. But what will it be like for new board members? That will be an increasing issue and the 'on-boarding process' (hideous jargon) will need to take this into account.

In Ministry of Defence meetings, video works well for operational decision-making, but poorly for policy development.

Virtual meetings ALWAYS seem to start late. For my team meetings – of around 25 people – I even have my assistant send a reminder to everyone the day before with the agenda asking that people join a few minutes before the hour to ensure we begin promptly. But there are *always* at least two or three people that have tech challenges (or at least say that they do!) so we always seem to start late. I guess there are a couple of options – start at the scheduled time anyway even if people are still joining, or factor that inevitable five minute delay into the agenda. I tend to do the latter.

It depends on the meeting, but meeting attendees can be so much more easily distracted on virtual meetings than they would be IRL. Some are subtle about doing emails (i.e. while staring at the Zoom screen), but others don't seem to care and are openly working on a second screen – I've even seen people take calls (while on mute). I get very irritated by that and I know it annoys others! When it's appropriate I start the meeting by asking for everyone's attention throughout and saying how much the meeting will benefit from everyone being engaged ... but still, some people don't have any qualms about how they appear. I had one chap sloppily eating an ice cream cone the other day while we were looking at the Q3 financial forecast. Odd – you wouldn't do that IRL, so why do it on Zoom!?

Another curveball for a chair in the virtual world is around the identity of participants ... take the time for introductions around the virtual table.

My experience of virtual chairing is that it is very efficient but not very bonding .... Zoom doesn't encourage conversation .... Much look forward to getting back to non-virtual!

LAST WORDS, WORDS, WORDS

What is so persuasive about these voices from different virtual chairs and different people being virtually chaired around the world is the high level of agreement as to the key issues. And the key issues are ones that have surfaced regularly for the chairing of physical meetings – preparation, practice, one conversation, inclusiveness, energy, importance of the secretariat/PAs. But it is early days for virtual chairing.

As this book was going to press, I attended via Zoom the AGM of a professional association with members taking part from around the world. One year before, the AGM had taken place in a hotel in Prague at the end of the annual conference. Around 30 people attended both events – many of them regular AGM attenders, knowing each other well.

Compared with the physical AGM the year before, and despite the same experienced and energetic chair who chaired both AGMs, the whole event lacked warmth, spontaneity, enjoyment. It was very functional, got through the business quickly, but felt wooden. It lacked creativity. It lacked serendipity, the benefit of chance encounters. There was no conversation as such. And certainly no conversation over the coffee before or afterwards.

RESEARCH FINDINGS ON VIRTUAL MEETINGS

A team of academics in Cambridge, Massachusetts has been exploring the impact of Covid on employees' virtual meeting experiences through a study of lockdowns in 16 large metropolitan areas in North America, Europe and the Middle East.

> [W]e find, compared to pre-pandemic levels, increases in the number of meetings per person (+12.9 percent) and the number of attendees per meeting (+13.5 percent), but decreases in the average length of meetings (-20.1 percent). Collectively, the net effect is that people spent less time in meetings per day (-11.5 percent) in the post-lockdown period.[1]

I do hope that *The Economist's* Bartleby and Simon Jenkins, cited at the start of this book, would be pleased. Thanks to the brave new world of virtual chairing, people are spending 11.5 percent less time in meetings!

Opportunity Cost. Productivity. Hope.

"Had we but world enough and time …." Andrew Marvell (1681).[2]

REFERENCES

1. DeFilippis, E., Impink, S.M., Singell, M., Polzer, J.T. and Sadun, R. (July 2020), "Collaborating During Coronavirus: The Impact of COVID-19 on the Nature of Work", *National Bureau of Economic Research Working Paper No. 27612*.

2. Marvell, A. (1681), "To His Coy Mistress", www.poetryfoundation.org.